American Pottery Wall Pockets

Mark Bassett

4880 Lower Valley Road, Atglen, PA 19310 USA

Copyright © 2004 by Mark Bassett
Library of Congress Control Number: 2003112959

All rights reserved. No part of this work may be reproduced or used in any form or by any means—graphic, electronic, or mechanical, including photocopying or information storage and retrieval systems—without written permission from the publisher.

The scanning, uploading and distribution of this book or any part thereof via the Internet or via any other means without the permission of the publisher is illegal and punishable by law. Please purchase only authorized editions and do not participate in or encourage the electronic piracy of copyrighted materials.

"Schiffer," "Schiffer Publishing Ltd. & Design," and the "Design of pen and ink well" are registered trademarks of Schiffer Publishing Ltd.

Designed by Joseph M. Riggio Jr.
Type set in Humanist 521 BT/Humanist 521 BT

ISBN: 0-7643-1975-2
Printed in China
1 2 3 4

Published by Schiffer Publishing Ltd.
4880 Lower Valley Road
Atglen, PA 19310
Phone: (610) 593-1777; Fax: (610) 593-2002
E-mail: Info@schifferbooks.com
For the largest selection of fine reference books on this and related subjects, please visit our web site at
www.schifferbooks.com
We are always looking for people to write books on new and related subjects. If you have an idea for a book please contact us at the above address.

This book may be purchased from the publisher.
Include $3.95 for shipping.
Please try your bookstore first.
You may write for a free catalog.

In Europe, Schiffer books are distributed by
Bushwood Books
6 Marksbury Ave.
Kew Gardens
Surrey TW9 4JF England
Phone: 44 (0)20-8392-8585
Fax: 44 (0)20-8392-9876
E-mail: info@bushwoodbooks.co.uk
Free postage in the UK. Europe: air mail at cost

Contents

Introduction 4
Chapter 1. Wall Pockets through the Years 6
Chapter 2. American Art Pottery Wall Pockets 9
Chapter 3. Undocumented Wall Pockets 127
Chapter 4. Other Hanging Items 133
Chapter 5. Factory Marks 146
Selected Bibliography 156
Index 160

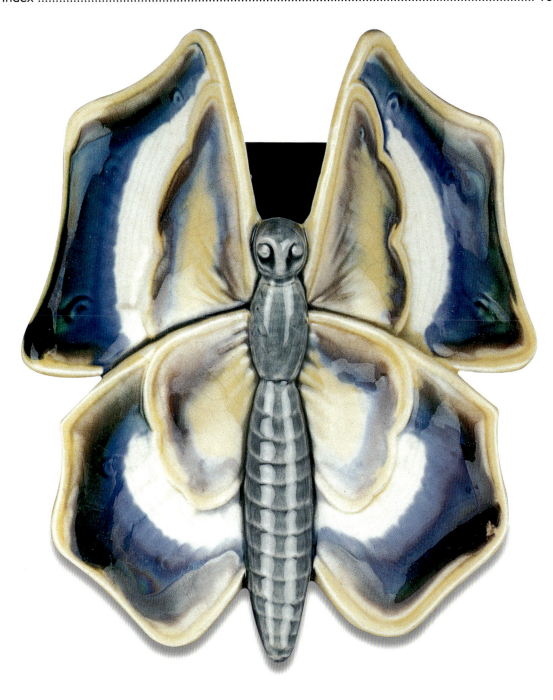

Introduction

American Art Pottery Wall Pockets illustrates the products of over sixty American makers of artistic and collectible wall pockets—vases made to hang on the wall. Hundreds of beautiful photographs record the vivid glazes and imaginative shapes. Close-up photographs identify typical marks, and a selected bibliography points readers to more detailed information.

The Roseville and Weller sections of this book depict nearly all known wall pockets by the two highly collectible Zanesville, Ohio, firms. Also well represented are Brush-McCoy, Camark, Frankoma, Hull, Nelson McCoy, Peters & Reed, and Rookwood. No other book contains more wall pockets by Fulper, Grueby, Marblehead, Owens, or Teco. Among the Arts and Crafts era potteries are California Faience, Jervis, Newcomb Pottery, George E. Ohr, Overbeck, Strobl, Walley, and Wheatley. The book also features wall pockets by less familiar concerns—from Alamo to Western Stoneware.

Definitions

The term *wall pocket* (or *wall vase*) refers to a vase made to hang on the wall. Most pottery wall pockets have a flat undecorated side and one or more holes to allow hanging on a nail. (Factory-made hanging holes are glazed on the inside.) The back of a *corner wall pocket* features two flat surfaces that meet at a right angle, so that it can be hung in the corner of a room. Some wall pockets are meant to be hung by their handles.

In addition to wall pockets, many collectors also seek hanging items originally made for a different purpose. (An assortment of these shapes is illustrated in Chapter 4.) Reference books on wall pockets often include examples of these shape families, in addition to wall vases.

Unlike bowls or floor tiles—which fulfill a basic need in the homes—wall pockets are not required for a household to function smoothly. Their appeal is primarily aesthetic, even though they can be used to hold cut flowers or potted plants. In this respect, any wall pocket satisfies a basic tenet of the Arts and Crafts Movement—namely, John Ruskin's admonition that the objects in one's home should be beautiful as well as useful.

Although the title of this book includes the term *American art pottery*, some items shown here would be more accurately described as "artware" or "novelties." As Marion John Nelson notes in *Art Pottery of the Midwest* (1988), the term *art pottery* generally refers to "decorative ware produced to a greater or lesser degree by hand after 1870 as a reaction against machine culture and nineteenth-century materialism" (page 1).

The role of hand decoration and craftsmanship varied from one firm to the next. As Nelson observes, "The methods of mass production rapidly gained ground in the making of art pottery." Even before 1910, molds were employed—instead of the potter's wheel—at art potteries like Fulper, Rookwood, Teco, and Van Briggle. For decades after the Arts and Crafts Movement reached its zenith (around 1915), many American potteries continued to emphasize glaze chemistry and design. These complications make it difficult, even for a historian, to explain precisely how art pottery differs from what Paul Evans calls "industrial artware."

American Art Pottery Wall Pockets is an illustrated survey of both handmade and cast wares made primarily between 1900 and the present. Each company's products are shown in roughly chronological order. This arrangement encourages comparison and demonstrates the ingenuity of American potters in inventing and reinventing the concept of the "wall pocket." Some motifs and decorative techniques recur in a later generation; others turn out to be specific to a particular time or maker.

Reproductions

Some shapes and glazes were popular enough that makers mimicked one another. In recent years, vintage designs have been reproduced in clumsily constructed versions—and often marked in a manner that imitates the original product. When possible, *American Art Pottery Wall Pockets* includes notes about shapes that have been reproduced by others. For a recommended source of information about (and photographs of) recent reproductions of McCoy, Roseville, and other vintage wall pockets, visit *www.ohioriverpottery.com* on the Internet.

Some reproductions are close enough to the originals that their presence in the marketplace can (at least temporarily) lower values. To cite one instance: During the late 1980s and early 1990s, potter J.D. James made "retro" (that is, reproduction) versions of most Hull *Bow-Knot* items, including their original marks. Although his *Bow-Knot* lookalikes are no longer in production, Hull collectors still debate how to distinguish an original Hull piece from a J.D. James example. (On the telephone with me, J.D. James explained that his standard procedure is to add hand-incised marks reading "J.D. James" or "by J.D.," but some buyers specifically requested examples that had no mark other than the vintage Hull marks.) For information about J.D. James' current work, visit *www.potterybyjd.com*.

Values

Values are a product of such influences as condition, decorative value (including artistic or technical sophistication), historical importance, market supply and demand, provenance, and size. Some of these influences are variable—for example, as fashions change or new marketplaces emerge. The subject of valuation is complicated enough that among seasoned buyers there can be widely divergent opinions of the value of a particular piece. The same is true of appraisers. Valuation is always an art as much as (or perhaps more than) a science.

Condition is always an important consideration. Distracting factory flaws, chips, hairline cracks, and restoration all lower the market value of a piece of pottery. When condition issues are present, items that typically sell in mint condition for $250–500 can easily bring only 50 to 75% of that amount. When damaged, a $50 wall pocket can prove difficult to sell at $20. At the other extreme, rare wall pockets—those valued over $1000 in mint condition—can sometimes bring prices near their "full value," even with damage or factory flaws.

Some variables that affect value are specific to a particular company's products and/or collectors. Collectors of Abingdon rate the limited-production (early) colors more highly than later glazes or glazes used for many years. Most Roseville and Brush McCoy collectors pay a higher price for a blue example than for a brown example of the same shape. In contrast, Rookwood and Nelson McCoy collectors pay less attention to color variations. In *American Art Pottery Wall Pockets*, the values refer *only* to the particular color variation illustrated. For more information about how color variations affect value, readers should consult an appropriate book listed in the Selected Bibliography.

Today an important influence on buyers and sellers is the Internet. Both on-line antique shops and auction sites like *eBay.com*™ are changing our ideas about rarity, selection, and value. Collectors assembling a "complete" collection of one company's products may have paid a higher price than is necessary today to obtain a specific shape.

There are other pressures to consider. In an uncertain economic climate, antique dealers can feel pressured to sell because of sluggish sales. Some think it a wise business practice, in any season, to "move" inventory (by lowering the asking price) and thereby keep their booths looking fresh to potential buyers. Fads among buyers come and go, making an item or company "hot" for a time and temporarily affecting market values. Widely anticipated books and exhibitions can also affect value. People who live near a pottery site may find rare items priced much higher (or common ones priced much lower) than buyers in other parts of the country experience.

The estimated values cited here are *not* intended as appraisals of the collections I was fortunate to be able to photograph. Instead, my goal was to approximate the *fair market value*—the price at which a typical and knowledgeable buyer and seller might agree to a transaction, assuming that there is no particular pressure on either person to buy or to sell the piece that day. *The values in this book are intended merely as a guide. Neither the author nor the publisher can accept responsibility for losses (or gains) experienced as a result of reading this book.*

Acknowledgments

Several long-time collectors of wall pockets allowed me to photograph their collections for this book, and their generosity is much appreciated. These include Stan and Nancy Gracyalny; Douglas and Barbara Grant; Mark and Barb Harris; Gordon and Sue Hoppe; James Johnson; Jeff Koehler Real Estate & Auction Company (Zanesville, Ohio); Joanne and Glenn Lindberg; Kendall Scally; Mike and Leita Schultz; Raymond F. and Elain Stoll; Vickie Surry; and Joe and Betty Yonis. The items shown in this book as being from the "Lindberg collection" were sold at auction in July 2002 by Jeff Koehler Real Estate & Auction Company (Zanesville, Ohio). For allowing me to photograph wall pockets being offered for sale, I must also thank JoAnn and Bill Harrison; Vera Kaufman, Buried Treasures/Vintage Vera (Manchester, New Hampshire); Mike McAllister, McAllister Auctions (Grand Ledge, Michigan); Mike Nickel and Cynthia Horvath (Portland, Michigan); and Chester Sturm, Fiesta Antiques.

For information about Chinese porcelain wall pockets, and for permission to publish one of their photographs, I thank June and Robert Grasso, Kyoto Antiques (Boston, Massachusetts). While studying the subject of early American majolica wall pockets, I received assistance from members of the International Majolica Society (*www.majolicasociety.com*), including Pam Ferrazzutti; Duane and Wanda Matthes, *www.eMajolica.com;* and Mary R. (Polly) Wilbert. Thanks to author Jeffrey B. Snyder for permission to reprint a photograph from his book *Marvelous Majolica*. I would also like to thank artist Michael Hartnett (Michael Harnett Art Studio, Stanhope, New Jersey) for allowing me to publish two of his photographs of miniature wall pockets that he designed and produced in his studio. Thanks to Ephraim Faience Pottery (Deerfield, Wisconsin) for permission to publish a photograph of their latest handmade wall pocket, and to Gordon Hoppe and Robert Seery for their photographs of wall pockets in their collections. My gratitude also goes to Ann Gilbert McDonald for reviewing the Weller section of this book.

To estimate current values, I read the most recent price guides (see bibliography) and reviewed eBay™ and live auction results. In addition to the approximations of value graciously provided by those whose pottery I photographed, I would also like to thank the following collectors and dealers for their assistance with this subject: Linda Carrigan; Mark and Marie Latta; Dave Johnson and Collette Lnenicka; Mrs. Robert Ross; and Allan Wunsch. For some examples, values were not available; in those instances, the abbreviation "NPD" (meaning "no price determined") is used.

Chapter 1
Wall Pockets through the Years

During the late nineteenth century, in both England and the U.S., hanging match holders and magazine racks were offered to the public in materials such as wood, metal, glass, wicker, linen, and crocheted twine. The 1897 and 1902 Sears, Roebuck and Co. catalogs included rectangular framed prints, called "wall pockets," which could be tilted forward, held secure by a metal chain, to hold "papers, magazines, etc." or, when placed near a piano or pump organ, sheet music (see Newbound 174). According to Fredda Perkins, some of the latter designs held a specially fabricated metal planter behind the print: "A landscape might then have actual greenery spilling from around the frame" (page 7). Perkins theorizes that the late Victorian "interest in bringing nature indoors may have led to the manufacture of decorative containers designed specifically to allow plants to become a decoration for the wall."

Victorian Period

Decorated porcelain wall pockets probably originated in China, where examples are known to date to the mid- to late 1700s. It is not clear who made the first pottery wall pockets—or whether these novelties first emerged in the U.S. or abroad. Between about 1880 and 1910, at least three Virginia folk potters in the Shenandoah Valley produced handmade stoneware wall pockets with applied flowers and/or birds (see Wiltshire 72, 98, 104). Also during the late 1800s, decorated pottery wall vases were made in England by several Devonshire potteries. Another early American wall pocket, made with a mold, is a ca. 1882–1890 majolica butterfly by Griffen, Smith and Hill, of Phoenixville, Pennsylvania. This now rare design appears to be the only wall pocket produced by an American maker that specialized in majolica.

China, ca. 1736–1795. Pair, 7.25" wall pockets, decorated porcelain, unmarked. *Photograph by June Grasso, Kyoto Antiques (Boston, Massachusetts).* $800–900

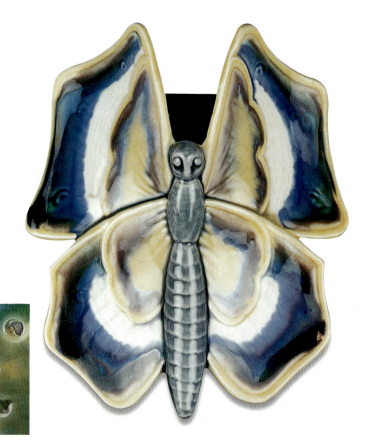

Griffen, Smith and Hill (Phoenixville, Pennsylvania), ca. 1882–1890. Wall pocket, butterfly, die-impressed GSH monogram and ETRUSCAN. *Reprinted with permission from Jeffrey B. Snyder, Marvelous Majolica: An Easy Reference and Price Guide (Atglen, Pennsylvania: Schiffer, 2001), page 80.* $3000–4000

Ephraim Faience (Deerfield, Wisconsin, 2003.) 8.25" leaf wall pocket, shape 320, die impressed logo and shape number. *Courtesy of Ephraim Faience Pottery.* $100-125.

About 1881 Rookwood Pottery (of Cincinnati) introduced shape 134, a hanging soap cup (Peck II, page 52). Designed in May 1886, that influential company's first wall pocket (shape 287) was a vase with a strap-like handle to allow hanging, copied from an object in the Metropolitan Museum of Art. In August 1892 a rectangular wall pocket with foliate trim was introduced (shape 661). Sometime between 1896 and 1902, the J.B. Owens Pottery (Zanesville, Ohio) produced a bamboo-shaped wall pocket with underglaze slip decoration (see page 53).

The Arts and Crafts Era

In 1903 Rookwood introduced a historically important group of wall pockets in the Arts and Crafts and Art Nouveau styles, some floriform, and often glazed in matt green or hand decorated. During those years Rookwood products were studied closely and quickly imitated by Zanesville-area potteries. By 1905 Owens, Roseville, and Weller had all added wall pockets to their lines.

First Weller offered a peacock feather-shaped wall pocket as part of their 1904 *Art Nouveau* line. In 1905, figural shapes characterized some of Roseville's wall pockets and other hanging items, many glazed in an organic, heavily textural *Matt Green*. Owens wall pockets were often glazed in either matte green or a metallic bronze. In 1907 the Owens Pottery was devastated by a major fire and never fully recovered. That year Weller introduced *Souevo*, a pattern imitating Native American wares; some wall pockets were made in *Matt Green*. Other companies who probably produced wall pockets before 1910 include Cambridge, Grueby, Jervis, Newcomb Pottery, George Ohr, Strobl, Walley, and Wheatley.

By 1916 the three Ohio firms Rookwood, Roseville, and Weller had produced dozens of wall pockets—some cone-shaped, some decorated with low-relief flowers or leaves. About that time, Rookwood introduced four faience wall pockets decorated in polychrome—featuring two satyrs, a rook, and a squirrel. Among its many new designs, Roseville offered cherub-decorated *Donatello* designs and a rectangular *Creamware* wall pocket featuring satirical, hand-colored drawings called *Tourist*. Weller wall pockets of those years included shapes in the *Burntwood, Ivory,* and *Roma* lines.

The popularity of American art pottery wall pockets reached such a peak that Clarence Moores Weed opened the January 1916 installment of his "Garden and Orchard" column for *House Beautiful* with a discussion titled "The Useful Wall-Pockets." Among his illustrations was a *Matt Green* example of Roseville's hemispherical shape 1205, planted with jonquils and decorated with impressed geometric lines (see page 75).

Observing that crowded window sills detract from one's enjoying the beauty of line and color in living plants, Weed noted that pottery manufacturers were offering a "great variety of designs of the so-called wall-pockets intended for use on walls or other vertical surfaces" (page xvi). Such products were being offered for sale, Weed explained, "by the better shops and department stores of the larger cities, as well as in the catalogues of the more important seed- and plant-houses."

Weed cautioned his readers: "In selecting [wall pockets] one should remember that … the lines and colors of leaves and flowers are to be the chief attraction … the eye of the observer should not be led away to the brilliance of the container. Subdued color tones are to be desired." Although wall pockets were "primarily designed to hold cut flowers," Weed advised readers, "many of them are just as desirable as receptacles for growing plants. Even though drainage is impracticable one can with a little care in watering keep a great variety of foliage and flowering plants thriving in them."

Weed recommended various plants for growing in a wall pocket, including "climbing or drooping vines" like "the German Ivy, the English Ivy, and the Madeira vine… The long branches with their decorative leaves hang from the rim of the receptacle in a way to make an attractive display against the plain background of the wall. In a sunny room, opening southward, one can even grow the lovely Japanese morning glories from seed and bring them into blossom…."

Other possibilities included foliage plants like *Tradescantia* and asparagus fern, as well as daffodils, hyacinths, and other spring-flowering bulbs. Of the bulb flowers, Weed counseled homeowners that "the Paper-white Narcissus and the Chinese Lily Narcissus may be grown in them from the start so that the whole process of growth may be watched from day to day. Others, like the Daffodils, Dutch Hyacinths, Jonquils, and others should be started in flower-pots and left in a cool room for root growth. Then they may be planted in the wall-pockets. One of the best ways is to start the bulbs in paper flower-pots and set pot and all in the receptacle on the wall" (page xvii).

Weed concluded this discussion with a general commentary:

> Very attractive combinations of plant and picture may be made by hanging the wall-pockets in connection with appropriate Japanese prints. In this way one can bring into our American homes a suggestion of that charming custom of the Japanese by which a flower or a picture or both hold for a brief time the place of honor in the living-room, generally with a suggestion of the spirit of the season in the outer world.
>
> Care must of course be taken in watering plants in these wall-pockets to see that no injurious spots mar the background. The best way is to remove the receptacles from the wall when water is to be added and then to wipe them off carefully before replacing them.

Modern and Contemporary Wall Pockets

Between 1916 and 1930 the list of American companies producing wall pockets came to include Brush, California Faience, Camark, Cowan, Fulper, Haeger, Hampshire, Marblehead, Paul Revere/Saturday Evening Girls, Peters and Reed, Red Wing, Robinson Ransbottom, and Van Briggle. The 1930s and 1940s welcomed into that specialty such firms as Abingdon, Cliftwood, Frankoma, Hull, Lenox, Muncie, Nelson McCoy, Niloak, and Western Stoneware. Long after Roseville ceased operations in 1954—the mid-point of a postwar era that also saw the closing of Weller and Rookwood—American art pottery wall pockets were still being produced by Hyalyn and by numerous small makers in California and elsewhere. For histories of these and other American potteries, see the Selected Bibliography.

In 2004, more than a century after the first American art pottery wall pockets were produced, new wall pockets are still being made by small potteries. The techniques and decorative motifs used by these entrepreneurs vary as widely as their formal art education and experience in ceramics. Among the new designs found on Internet searches when this book was being written: planter-shaped wall pockets with an applied bee, shell, or starfish by Clay Trout Pottery (Mattapoisett, Massachusetts); heart-shaped wall pockets by Sunrise Pottery (San Antonio, Texas); and unglazed red terra cotta wall pockets known as Tecate Pottery Novelty items, made by Pottery Manufacturing and Distributing (previously C.E. Jones Ceramics, Gardena, California). By early 2001, the well-known Ephraim Faience Pottery (Deerfield, Wisconsin) had retired two wall pockets that were formerly part of their line—a Grueby-style floral and one with a medium-relief dragonfly. Their Catalog Number 8 (2003) includes shape 320, a leaf wall pocket glazed in a rich semi-gloss green.

Today among the dozens of American studio potters producing one-of-a-kind, wheel-thrown or hand-sculpted wall pockets are Bruen Pottery (distributed by Two Hundred Hands, Albuquerque, New Mexico); The Clay Place (Sicklerville, New Jersey); Hannah Hunter (offered by Arts Prescott, Prescott, Arizona); Joy Imai (studio at Allied Arts Guild, Menlo Park, California); Pine Hollow Pottery (Delmont, Pennsylvania); Carolyn Rice Art Pottery (Lilburn, Georgia); and Toby Rosenberg, rara avis designs (Portland, Maine). Intrigued by the technical challenge and inspired by the artistry of Roseville and other vintage wall pockets, Michael Hartnett (Michael Hartnett Art Studio, Stanhope, New Jersey) has made a variety of miniature wall pockets for his private collection.

Vintage Roseville *Futura* Wall Pocket and Miniature. *Photograph by Michael Harnett, Michael Harnett Art Studio, Stanhope, New Jersey.* NPD

Vintage Roseville *Blackberry* Wall Pocket and Miniature. *Photograph by Michael Harnett, Michael Harnett Art Studio, Stanhope, New Jersey.* NPD

The continuing interest in wall pockets has also prompted a number of U.S. companies to import pottery examples from other countries, often without a permanent factory mark. To the beginner, some of these products can be mistaken for vintage majolica pieces. Other firms are manufacturing wall pockets from non-ceramic materials like polyresin. These include the Mary Engelbreit line (St. Louis; distributed through Florida Plants, Ft. Lauderdale, Florida) and the products of the imprecisely named firm "Hines Pottery" (wholesale only, Houston, Texas).

Chapter 2
American Art Pottery Wall Pockets

This chapter features wall pockets by more than sixty American potteries, arranged alphabetically by maker. Each company's products are shown roughly in chronological order, with dates and line names based on current research. For some companies, it is possible to gain a panoramic and historic overview of their products.

In *Introducing Roseville Pottery* (1997), new research finally allowed collectors and historians to construct an accurate chronology for Roseville's over 130 lines. More new findings were published in *Bassett's Roseville Prices* (1999) and in *Understanding Roseville Pottery* (2002). (By 2003, revised 2nd editions of two of these volumes were already in print.) As a result, the Roseville sections of *American Art Pottery Wall Pockets* are both comprehensive and accurate. (Revised editions of the other Roseville books listed in the bibliography are sorely needed, incorporating the new research findings published in my books on Roseville.)

Today new research on Weller is also underway, an indication that our current understanding of that company is probably incomplete. In 2004 an important exhibition (documented in a detailed catalog) was staged at the Zanesville (Ohio) Art Center—*Weller Pottery: The Rare, the Unusual, the Seldom Seen,* by Linda Carrigan and Allan Wunsch. In addition, Ann Gilbert McDonald has continued her research on Weller and hopes to publish an entirely new book on Weller within the next few years. With assistance from Mike Nickel, the Huxfords have revised their Weller book to eliminate items no longer thought to be Weller products. Photography for my forthcoming book *Introducing Weller Pottery* is underway, to be followed by several years of archival research and writing. (For information on my own Weller research, please visit www.markbassett.com. For these reasons, the Weller sections of this book—although second to the Roseville sections in length—are likely to be revised in later editions.

The Weller research projects are merely one circle within a large network of renewed interest among scholars in twentieth-century decorative arts. Today's researchers are striving to produce ever more accurate reference books about American art pottery. Through careful scholarship and judicious use of attribution and historical methods, they are revealing how many errors were made during the years when collectors were encouraged to document their collections by writing "reference guides." Each new scholarly publication reminds the author of a broadly focused work like *American Art Pottery Wall Pockets* that (as always) his conclusions are tentative.

Abingdon Potteries (Abingdon, Illinois), ca. 1930s–1940s. 8.75" wall pocket 377, *Morning Glory,* blue inkstamp mark, die-impressed 377; 7.75" x 8.75" wall pocket 375, *Double Morning Glory,* blue inkstamp mark. *Surry collection.* $40–50, $55–65. *Caution:* A Japanese reproduction of the wall pocket on the left is known (see Gibson, Book II, page 125).

Abingdon, 1948–1950. 5.5" x 8" wall pocket 640, *Triad*, blue inkstamp mark, die-impressed 640. *Surry collection*. $75–100

Alamo Pottery (San Antonio, Texas), late 1940s or early 1950s. 5.75" x 7.75" wall pocket 200, die-impressed 200. *Surry collection*. $40–50

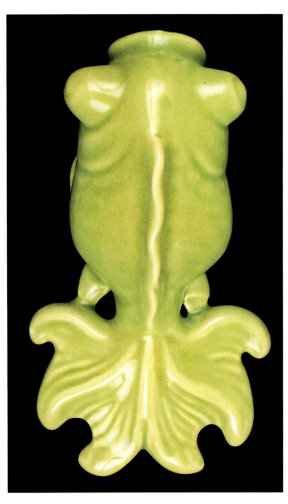

American Ceramic Products (Los Angeles, California) *La Mirada*, ca. 1930s. 10" wall pocket, koi goldfish, unmarked. *Surry collection*. $100–125

Abingdon, 1948–1950. 8.75" x 7.625" wall pocket 648, *Acanthus*, die-impressed 648. *Surry collection*. $65–75

Brown County Pottery (Nashville, Tennessee), 1935; and **Brown County Hills Pottery** (Nashville, Tennessee), late 1950s or 1960s. Brown County 6.5" wall pocket, hand-incised "BROWN / COUNTY / POTTERY / 1935"; Brown County Hills 8.25" wall pocket, hand-painted "Brown County Hills / Pottery." *Scally collection.* $400–600, $300–400

Brown County Hills, late 1950s or 1960s. 6.5" wall pocket, hand-painted "Brown County / Hills Pottery" (script). *Grant collection.* $300–400

Brown County, 1930s. 5.25" x 6" wall pocket, hand-incised floral motifs, hand-incised Brown / County / Pottery (script). *Grant collection.* $850–1000. Because decorated Brown County pieces are very desirable, collectors are usually willing to overlook small chips or nicks.

Brush Pottery Co., or **Brush-McCoy Pottery Co.** (Roseville, Ohio), probably 1920s. Two 9.5" wall pockets, conical shell, shape 026, based on an Owens design, unmarked. *Grant collection.* $250–300 (each). For a vintage illustration showing several Owens look-alikes manufactured by Brush, see Sanford, Book 1, page 131.

Brush, 1929. 6" wall pocket, parrot, *Ivotint* glaze. *Surry collection.* $125–175

Brush, 1929. 6.5" wall pocket, *Roman*, die-impressed shape number (illegible), glazed in the style of *Ivoko* kitchenware. *Surry collection.* $125–150

Brush, 1929. 6" wall pocket, *Roman*, die-impressed 455. *Grant collection.* $100–125

Brush, 1930s. 8" wall pocket, *Roman*, brown *Onyx* glaze, die-impressed 455 / 7 2. *Surry collection.* $125–175 (or $150–200 in green, $175–250 in blue)

Brush, 1930. 8" wall pocket, *Wise Bird*, black inkstamp Brush Ware trademark. *Surry collection.* $275–350

Brush, 1956. 7.25" x 10.5" wall pocket 541, fish, die-impressed 541 / USA. *Surry collection.* $125–150

Brush, 1939. 6.25" wall pocket, unmarked. *Grant collection.* $100–125

Brush, 1956. 8" x 7.5" wall pocket 542, boxer, unmarked. *Surry collection.* $175–225. There is also a smaller version of this wall pocket, valued at $125–175.

California Art Products, Inc. (Los Angeles, California), late 1940s. 7.5" wall pocket, die-impressed Orchid / California / Arts; 7.5" wall pocket, die-impressed "Castor Bean" / California / Arts. *Surry collection.* $100–125 (each). The company name was identified in Gibson, Book II, pages 24–25.

California Arts, late 1940s. *Top:* 6" wall pocket, die-impressed "Lotus" / California / Arts. *Bottom:* 8.5" wall pocket, die-impressed "Iris" / California / Arts; 9.75" wall pocket, die-impressed "Calla Lily" / © '45 / Leyden – / Arts / California. *Surry collection.* $100–125 (each)

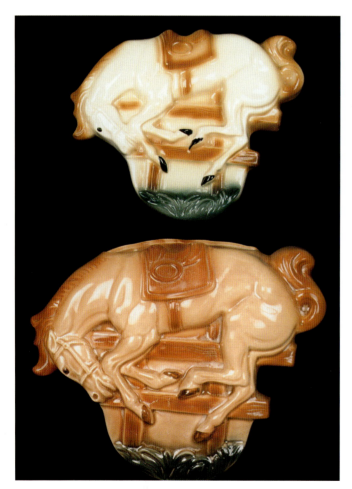

Brush, ca. 1950s. *Top:* 7" t. x 8.5" wall pocket 801, bucking horse, die-impressed 801 / USA. *Bottom:* 9" t. x 11.25" wall pocket, bucking bronco, unmarked. *Gracyalny collection.* $150–200, $200–250

Burley and Winter Pottery (Crooksville, Ohio), 1930s. 5.75" wall pocket 402, strawberry jar, die-impressed BURLEY-WINTER / CROOKSVILLE, O. / 402. *Surry collection.* $150–200

Camark, ca. 1926–1928. *Jeanne Conventional* 8" wall pocket, ca. 1927–1928, gold paper Arkansas label, gilt inkstamp mark in shape of Arkansas and reading GENUINE CAMARK; *Old English (Gray Blue)* 7.75" wall pocket, ca. 1926, hand-painted Lessell; *Silver Luster* 8.5" wall pocket, ca. 1927–1928, hand-painted LE CAMARK. *Grant collection*. $850–1000 (each). These floral and scenic motifs are hand painted in metallic lustres.

California Faience Co. (Berkeley, California), 1920s. 9.5" wall pocket, bird, die-impressed mark (script). *Surry collection*. $550–650

Camark, ca. early 1930s. *Aztec Red Mottled* 8.25" wall pocket, paper Arkansas label with notation "shape 166"; *Matt and Bright Combination Colors* 7.25" wall pocket, unmarked; *Matt and Bright Combination Colors* 8.25" wall pocket, gilt lettering COMPLIMENTS / OF / CHAMBER OF COMMERCE / CAMDEN, ARK. *Grant collection*. $500–600, $400–500, $500–600

Camark Pottery (Camden, Arkansas), ca. 1927–1928. 7.75" x 4" wall pocket, hand-painted iris, coralene-decorated background, unmarked. *Grant collection*. $750–850. The techniques used to decorated this wall pocket were developed about 1905 by John Lessell, for Owens' *Opalesce Inlaid* line. Comparable products were made at Fraunfelter China and Weller too, where Lessell also worked as a designer.

Camark, 1930s. *Green and Blue Mottled* 8.5" wall pocket, unmarked. *Grant collection.* $350–450

Camark, 1930s. 5.25" x 5.75" wall pocket, die-impressed CAMARK. *Surry collection.* $150–200

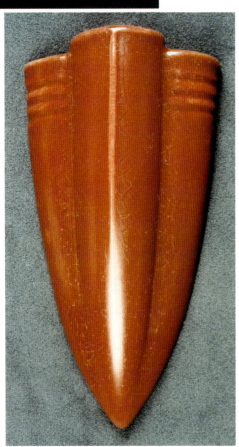

Camark, 1930s. 9.5" wall pocket, hand-incised A-18, pale buff clay. *Surry collection.* $250–300. For an example of this shape with an inkstamp CAMARK mark, see Gibson, Book II, page 223.

Camark, 1940s, *bas-relief iris*. 9.25" wall pocket, paper label, notations reading Shape 851, Finish R. *Surry collection.* $350–450. The bas-relief iris wall pockets are hand decorated. They are difficult to find in undamaged condition.

Camark, 1940s, *bas-relief iris*. 9.25" wall pocket, unmarked. *Grant collection*. $350–450

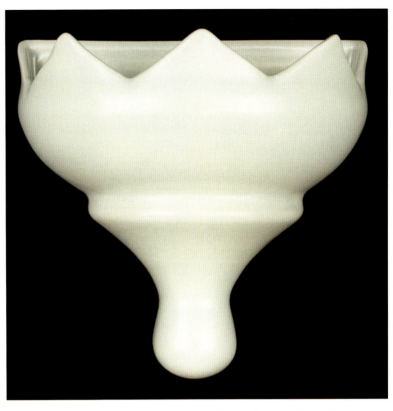

Camark, 1950s. 5" wall pocket, die-impressed Camark / USA / N22. *Surry collection*. $100–125

Camark, 1940s, *bas-relief iris*. 9.25" wall pocket, paper label. *Grant collection*. $350–450

Oakwood Pottery (Dayton, Ohio), ca. 1904, and **Cambridge Art Pottery** (Cambridge, Ohio), ca. 1907-1910. Oakwood, 11" x 8.5" wall pocket, die-impressed acorn logo; Cambridge (attribution), 11.25" wall pocket, unmarked. *Grant collection*. $400–500, $300–400. For information on Oakwood, see Lehner (page 327) and Evans (pages 199-200).

Cambridge (attribtuion), ca. 1907-1910. 11" wall pocket, unmarked. *Grant collection*. $300–400

Cliftwood Art Potteries (Morton, Illinois), ca. 1930s. 8.5" wall pocket, *Blue Mulberry,* paper label with Aladdin lamp logo and reading Cliftwood / THE PRIDE OF ANY HOME. *Surry collection.* $60–75

Catalina Island Pottery (Santa Catalina Island, California), ca. early 1930s. 9" wall pocket, shell, unmarked. *Grant collection*. $600–700

Cliftwood, ca. 1930s. 7.25" wall pocket, ribbed, die-impressed 49. *Surry collection*. $60–75. According to Marvin and Joy Gibson, this shape was attributed to Cliftwood by Doris and Burdell Hall (see Gibson, Book I, page 249; and Gibson, Book II, pages 236–237).

Cordey China Co. (Trenton, New Jersey), ca. 1940s–1950s. 8.25" wall pocket (and head vase), blue hand-painted ink 881 / 37. *Grant collection.* $350–450

Cliftwood, ca. 1930s. 11" wall pocket, ribbed, die-impressed 49. *Surry collection.* $75–100

Cowan Pottery Co. (Rocky River, Ohio), 1920s. 10.75" x 10.25" "lion" wall pocket, shape 694, *Larkspur*, unmarked. *Grant collection.* $650–750

Cliftwood, ca. 1938–1940. 7.75" wall pocket; 5.5" x 8.75" wall pocket—both unmarked. *Grant collection.* $75–100 (each)

19

Cowan, 1920s. Two 8.5" wall pockets, shape 653—in *Larkspur* (black inkstamp reading COWAN) and *Marigold* (unmarked). *Grant collection*. $150–200 (each)

Creek Pottery (Checotah, Oklahoma), 1970s. 8" x 6" wall pocket, arrowhead, molded (raised relief) tepee / Creek, gold and black foil label in shape of arrow, reading Authentic / INDIAN POTTERY / Made in Checotah, Okla. 74426. *Surry collection*. $50–65. The reflections from my lights make this piece appear to have a hairline crack, but it is actually undamaged.

Cowan, 1920s. 12.5" "Oriental" wall pocket, shape 654, *Pine Green*, unmarked. *Bassett collection*. $1500–2000

Dadson (California), age unknown. 8.75" wall pocket, die-impressed DADSON CALIF. 9. *Surry collection*. $35–45. This concern is not mentioned in Chipman or Lehner. For the original Weller shape on which this example is based, see page 113.

Diamond Pottery Corp. (Crooksville, Ohio), 1950s. 4.25" wall pocket, teapot, die-impressed DIAMOND POTTERY / CORPORATION / © / MADE IN USA. *Yonis collection.* $30–40

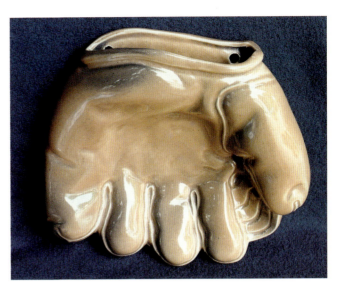

John E. Duffina (Los Angeles, California), ca. 1950s. 6.25" x 7" wall pocket, catcher's mitt, round inkstamp reading JOHN E. DUFFINA / © / LOS ANGELES / CALIFORNIA, U.S.A. *Mark Bassett Antiques, Lakewood, OH.* $35–45

Dryden Pottery (Ellsworth, Kansas), 1940s or 1950s. 4.25" wall pocket, 4-H Club souvenir, unmarked. *Surry collection.* $50–60. This shape was attributed to Dryden in Gibson, Book II, pages 192–193.

Faenza Pottery (Chicago, Illinois), 1920s. 9.25" x 5" wall pocket; 13" wall pocket—both die-impressed FAENZA / POTTERY. *Grant collection.* $400–500, $300–400. Because Faenza products are not well documented, values can only be approximated. For a brief mention of this concern, see Evans, page 347.

Kay Finch Ceramics (Corona del Mar, California), 1950s. 7.5" x 9.5" wall pocket, die-impressed Kay Finch / Calif. *Grant collection.* $100–150

Frankoma, ca. 1942. 5" x 7.75" x 3.75" wall pocket 85, bird handles. *Private collection.* $125–175. Also finished on the back and capable of being used as a vase or planter, this example has a factory hole near the rim on three sides and one in the base. It is believed to be a wall pocket for use on the porch.

Frankoma Pottery (Sapulpa, Oklahoma), ca. 1942. 2.5" wall pocket, buff clay, unmarked. *Private collection.* $375–450. Based on a small mask of an African man.

Frankoma, ca. 1942. 5.75" x 5.25" wall pocket 193, ram. *Private collection.* $250–350

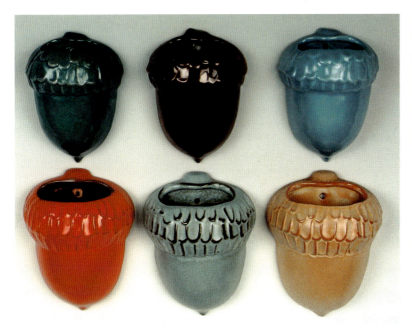

Frankoma, ca. 1940s or 1970s. 6" x 4.25" wall pocket 100 (left) and mask 100 (right), each hand-incised only SAI and 100. *Private collection.* $150–175, $45–55. These examples were made for Sigma Alpha Ipsilon, a sorority at the University of Oklahoma. If the mask has buff-colored clay, its value is about $100–150.

Frankoma, ca. 1942–1977. *Top:* Three 5.5" wall pockets 190, small acorn. *Bottom:* Three 6.25" wall pockets 190, large acorn. *Private collection. Top:* $75–85, $45–55, $55–65. *Bottom:* $75–85 (each). The larger size was made only during the 1960s.

Frankoma, ca. 1950s or 1960s. Three 5.5" wall pockets 190, small acorn. *Left:* Hand-painted pine cone motif, post-factory, refired, black ink signature "K Wetterberg / Colo." *Middle and right:* Custom designs for Order of Eastern Star, the middle example also lettered FANNIE McDOWELL, who was Worthy Grand Matron that year. *Private collection.* $65–75 (each)

Frankoma, ca. 1949–1953. Five 7" wall pockets 94Y, wagon wheels. *Private collection.* $75–100 (each)

Frankoma, ca. 1951. 2.75" x 4.5" wall pocket A1, die-impressed marks. *Surry collection*. $65–75. Frankoma catalogs describe this item as a "window pot with waterer." It has a flat base, allowing it to stand unsupported.

Frankoma, ca. 1950s and 1960s. 7" wall pocket, Billiken, die-impressed TULSA COURT / NO. 47 / R.O.J. (Royal Order of Jesters). *Private collection*. $150–200. The Billiken can bear various specially commissioned marks.

Frankoma, ca. 1951–1990s. Two 6.75" wall pockets 133, boot; 3.5" wall pocket 507S, small boot, reversed to show hole. *Surry collection*. $20–30, $10–15 (small), $20–30. The small boot was originally sold as a pair, with a leather thong to keep them together and to facilitate hanging. Value of pair: $20–30.

Frankoma, ca. 1964–1966. 10.75" x 12.75" wall pocket 196, leaves. *Private collection*. $225–275

Frankoma, ca. 1964–1966. Four 7.75" x 8.25" wall pockets 197, leaves. *Private collection.* $150–200 (each)

Frankoma, ca. 1972–1975, and 1999. Five 6.5" wall pockets 130, Phoebe. *Private collection. Top:* $75–85, $85–95. *Bottom:* $85–95, $100–125, $30–40. The bottom right example has a die-impressed date of 1999. Earlier examples of this shape—dating to ca. 1948–1952—are sometimes numbered 730 (instead of 130).

Frankoma, ca. 1974–1991. 8.75" wall pocket 913, Dutch shoe, die-impressed 913 only. *Surry collection.* $20–25

Frankoma Family Collectors Association. Eight 5.5" wall pockets, each die-impressed DESIGNED BY / Joniece Frank (script) / GLAZED & FIRED BY / FRANK X 2 / CAST BY / FRANKOMA / © FFCA. *Private collection.* $35–40 (each). These custom wall pockets were made as commemorative souvenirs for the 2000 (top) and 2001 (bottom) FFCA convention. For details, visit *www.frankoma.org*.

Fulper, ca. 1915 to early 1920s. 7" x 5.5" wall pocket, shape 481, black inkstamp FULPER. *Surry collection.* $400–500

Fulper Pottery (Flemington, New Jersey), ca. 1912 to early 1920s. Two 3.25" x 4.25" wall pockets—top with vertical "racetrack" FULPER inkstamp, and bottom with inkstamp reading RUST / CRAFT. *Grant collection.* $275–350, $375–450. The bottom example is believed to be an early piece.

Fulper, ca. 1915 to early 1920s. 11.75" wall pocket; 10.75" wall pocket; 10.75" wall pocket; 11.75" wall pocket. *Grant collection.* $700–800 (each). The far right example is unmarked; the other three are marked with a vertical "racetrack" FULPER inkstamp. The design in the middle is sometimes called "the Pipes of Pan."

Fulper, ca. 1915 to early 1920s. *Top:* Two 6.75" x 5.5" wall pockets, shape 481. *Bottom:* Three 8" x 4.5" wall pockets, shape 487. *Grant collection.* $400–500 (each), $500–600 (each). These five examples are marked with a vertical "racetrack" FULPER inkstamp. The bottom left example also has a paper label.

Fulper, ca. 1920s. Three 7.25" x 4.5" wall pockets, die-impressed 855—one (left) with the vertical "racetrack" FULPER inkstamp, and the others die-impressed FULPER. *Grant collection.* $500–600 (each)

Fulper, ca. 1925–1929. 8.75" corner wall pocket, fruit, shape 377, china body, vertical "racetrack" FULPER inkstamp. *Grant collection.* $300–400

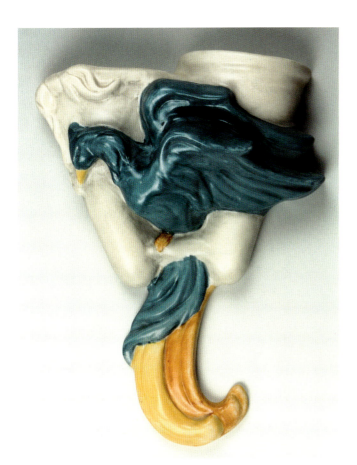

Fulper, ca. 1925–1929. 9.5" wall pocket, bird, shape 374, china body, vertical "racetrack" FULPER inkstamp. *Grant collection.* $600–700

Fulper, ca. 1920s. 7" x 8" wall pocket, die-impressed 856 / FULPER. *Grant collection.* $400–500

Fulper, ca. 1925–1929. Two 9.25" wall pockets, bird, china body, vertical "racetrack" FULPER inkstamp and black inkstamp 389. *Grant collection.* $400–500 (each)

Fulper *Fayence*, ca. 1925–1931. Two 10" wall pockets 961, bird, faience body, one (left) with hand-incised K and pencil notation 1-2025 / 85, the other unmarked. *Grant collection.* $250–300 (each). These glazes were called Colonial Blue and Silver Green.

Fulper *Fayence*, ca. 1925–1931. 7.75" wall pocket 997, fruit, faience body, paper label with hand-written notations "Fayence / 997 / Wall Pocket." *Grant collection.* $200–250

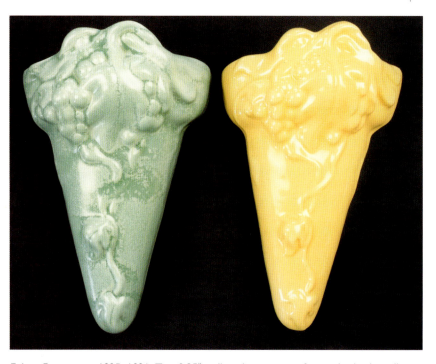

Fulper *Fayence*, ca. 1925–1931. Two 8.25" wall pockets, grapes, faience body, the yellow example bearing a paper label with hand-written notations "Fayence / #989 / Grape Wall Pocket." *Grant collection.* $200–250 (each). At Fulper, these glazes were called *Variegated Green Matte* and *Persian Yellow*. At Haeger, a similar mottled green glaze was called *Geranium Green*. Some shapes were probably made by both firms.

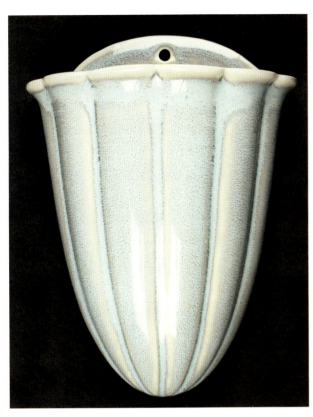

General Ceramics (New York, New York) *Carillon China*, 1930s or early 1940s. 7" wall pocket, black inkstamp CARILLON / (bell logo) / CHINA / U.S.A. *Bassett collection.* $75–100

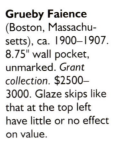

Grueby Faience (Boston, Massachusetts), ca. 1900–1907. 8.75" wall pocket, unmarked. *Grant collection.* $2500–3000. Glaze skips like that at the top left have little or no effect on value.

H.A. Graack (Silver Springs, Florida), ca. 1930s. 7" wall pocket, die-impressed SILVER SPRINGS, FLA. *Grant collection.* $150–200. Not knowing the name of this pottery, some refer to it as "Silver Springs" swirl ware.

Grueby, ca. 1900–1907. 7" x 5.25" wall pocket, unmarked. *Grant collection.* $1500–2000

Haeger, ca. 1930s. 6" wall pocket 128, unmarked. *Surry collection.* $125–150. This glaze was called *Geranium Green* at Haeger. A similar mottled green glaze by Fulper (and later, Stangl) was called *Variegated Green Matte* (for an example, see page 28).

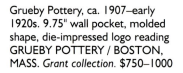

Grueby Pottery, ca. 1907–early 1920s. 9.75" wall pocket, molded shape, die-impressed logo reading GRUEBY POTTERY / BOSTON, MASS. *Grant collection.* $750–1000

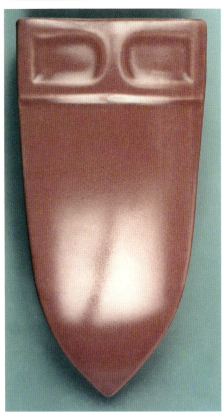

Haeger Potteries (Dundee, Illinois), ca. 1920s. 7" wall pocket 126, unmarked. *Surry collection.* $100–125

Haeger, ca. 1930s. Two 12" x 5.5" wall pockets, unmarked. *Grant collection.* $150–200 (each). This Teco-style wall pocket is Haeger shape E-194 (see Paradis, page 92).

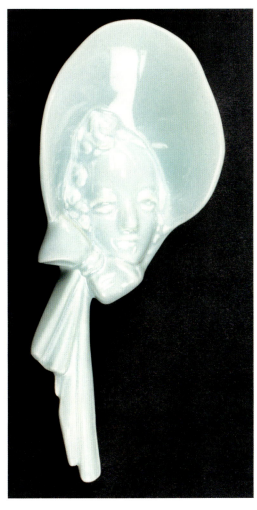

Haeger, ca. 1946. 10" wall pocket (and head vase) 3118, green and gold foil label. *Surry collection.* $100–125. This shape is difficult to find without damage.

Haeger, ca. late 1940s. 8.75" x 7" wall pocket, swan, Mauve Agate, die-impressed ROYAL HAEGER / R517 and USA. *Surry collection.* $175–250

Hammat Originals (Tulsa, Oklahoma), 1950s. 4" x 4.75" wall pocket, hand-incised Hammat Original (script). *Surry collection.* $50–75. This piece can also be used as a vase.

Hampshire Pottery (Keene, New Hampshire), ca. 1908–1914. 5.5" x 7" x 3.25" wall pocket, die-impressed Hampshire Pottery (script) and MO monogram (of designer Cadmon Robertson). *Grant collection.* $700–800

Hampshire, ca. 1908–1914. 7" x 5.25" wall pocket, leaves and buds, die-impressed Hampshire Pottery (script), OA, and MO monogram (of designer Cadmon Robertson). *Grant collection.* $1000–1200. This shape was derived from a Hampshire vase design.

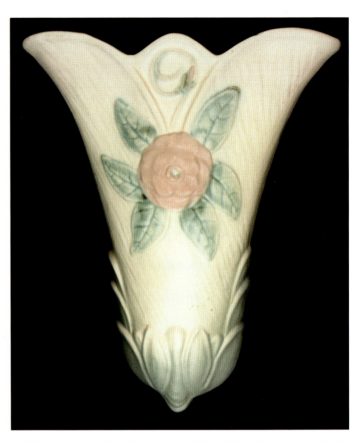

Hull *Open Rose* (or *Camellia*), ca. mid-1940s. 8.5" wall pocket, molded (raised relief) HULL / U.S.A. / 125-8 1/2 and hand-incised 21. *Yonis collection.* $400–500

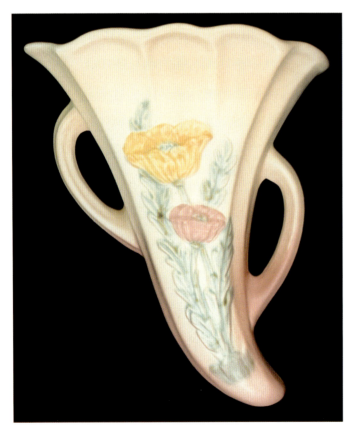

Hull Pottery (Crooksville, Ohio) *Poppy*, ca. mid-1940s. 9" wall pocket, molded (raised relief) HULL / U.S.A. / 609-9" and hand-incised 4. *Yonis collection.* $375–450

Hull *Rosella*, ca. 1946. Three 6.25" wall pockets, heart, molded (raised relief) Hull Art / U.S.A. / R-10-6 1/4". *Yonis collection.* $125–175 (each)

Hull *Bow-Knot*, ca. 1949. Two 8" wall pockets, whisk broom, die-impressed U.S.A / Hull Art / B-27-8". *Yonis collection.* $250–300 (each)

Hull *Sunglow*, ca. 1952. 6.75" wall pocket, cup and saucer, die-impressed U.S.A. / 80; 8.25" wall pocket, whisk broom, die-impressed U.S.A. / 82. *Yonis collection.* $100–150 (each)

Hull *Bow-Knot*, ca. 1949. Two 6" wall pockets, cup and saucer, die-impressed U.S.A. / Hull-Art / B-24-6. *Yonis collection.* $250–300 (each)

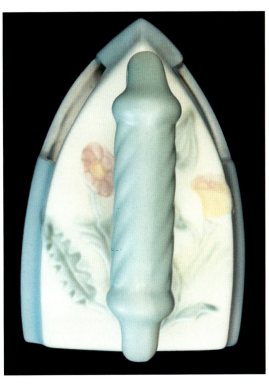

Hull *Bow-Knot*, ca. 1949. 6.25" wall pocket, iron, hand-incised 3. *Yonis collection.* $275–350

Hull *Bow-Knot*, ca. 1949. 6.25" wall pocket, iron, unmarked. *Yonis collection*. $275–350

Hull *Bow-Knot*, ca. 1949. 6" wall pocket, pitcher, molded (raised relief) U.S.A. / Hull Art / B-26-6 (on base). *Yonis collection*. $250–300

Hull *Bow-Knot*, ca. 1949. 6" wall pocket, pitcher, molded (raised relief) U.S.A. / Hull Art / B-26-6 (on base) and hand-incised 5. *Yonis collection*. $250–300

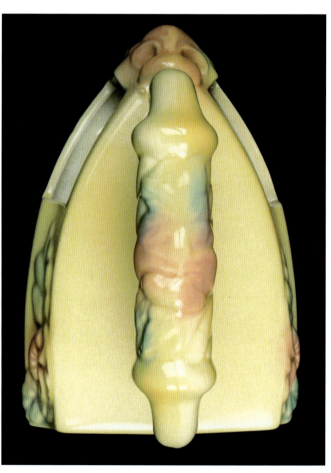

Hull *Sunglow*, ca. 1952. 6.25" wall pocket, iron, unmarked. *Yonis collection*. $100–150

Hull *Sunglow*, ca. 1952. 5.5" wall pocket, pitcher, trial (non-production) glaze, die-impressed U.S.A. / 81 on base. *Yonis collection*. $100–125 (in a production glaze). This example is difficult to value. On one hand, the trial glaze should increase value significantly; on the other hand, the piece is damaged, having a base chip and a cracked handle. Even in damaged condition, a trial-glaze Hull piece is usually worth at least twice the shape's value in a production glaze.

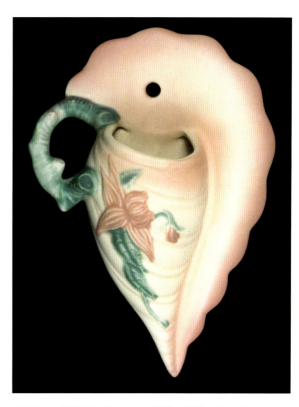

Hull *Post-1950 Woodland*, ca. 1950s. 7.5" wall pocket, molded (raised relief) W13-7 1/2" Hull (script) U.S.A. *Yonis collection*. $150–200

Hull *Woodland*, ca. 1949. 7.5" wall pocket, molded (raised relief) W13-7 1/2 Hull (script) U.S.A. *Yonis collection*. $200–250

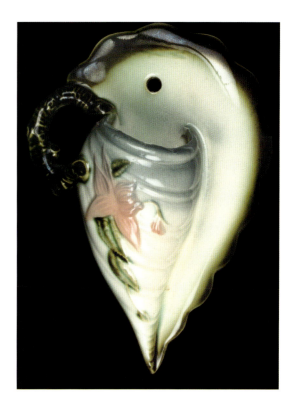

Hull *Two-Tone Woodland*, ca. 1950s. 7.5" wall pocket, molded (raised relief) W13-7 1/2" Hull (script) U.S.A. *Yonis collection*. $100–150

Hull *Royal Woodland,* ca. 1950s. Two 7.5" wall pockets, molded (raised relief) W13-7 1/2 Hull (script) U.S.A. *Yonis collection.* $75–100 (each)

Hull *Novelty,* ca. 1950s. 5.75" wall pocket, ribbon, die-impressed 71 – USA. *Yonis collection.* $45–60. This shape can also be used as a vase.

Hull *Novelty,* ca. 1950s. 6.25" wall pocket, goose, die-impressed Hull (script) / USA and 67. *Yonis collection.* $60–75. This shape can also be used as a vase.

Hull *Athena,* ca. 1970s. Two 8.25" wall pockets, picture frame, die-impressed 611 – U.S.A. *Yonis collection.* $100–150 (each). This shape can also be used as a vase.

Hyalyn Porcelain (Hickory, North Carolina), ca. 1948. 4.5" x 6.75" wall pocket, teapot, die-impressed hyalyn / 500/L, silver and brown paper label. *Surry collection.* $25–30

Indianapolis Terra Cotta Company (Indianapolis, Indiana), ca. 1920s. 7.25" wall pocket, Pharaoh, hand-incised "COMPLIMENTS OF IND TERRA COTTA CO." *Scally collection.* $400–500. Although this concern is not mentioned in Lehner, the company name was obtained from a fully marked example. This example is figural and also "crosses over" from the wall pocket category to interest collectors of advertising memorabilia and Egyptian motifs too.

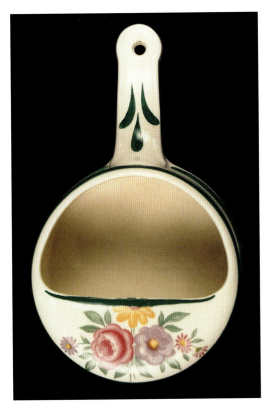

Hyalyn, ca. 1948. 9" wall pocket, skillet, molded (raised relief) hyalyn / 501. *Bassett collection.* $25–30

Hyalyn, ca. 1948–1958. *Top:* 7" Free Form wall pocket 325, 1951, die-impressed "hyalyn / 325"; 10.25" wall pocket 390, ca. 1958, die-impressed "USA / hyalyn (in oval) / 390"; 6.5" Golden Bars wall pocket 305, 1951, die-impressed "hyalyn / 305." *Bottom:* 11.75" wall pocket 510, hand decorated, ca. 1948, molded (raised relief) "hyalyn / 510." *Bassett collection.* $40–50, $30–40, $40–50, $25–30. For an interesting discussion of this firm, see Cliff R. Leonard and Duke Coleman, "H. Leslie Moody," pages 118–119 of Virginia Raymond Cummins, *Rookwood Pottery Potpourri* (1972; rpt. Cincinnati: Cincinnati Art Galleries, 1991).

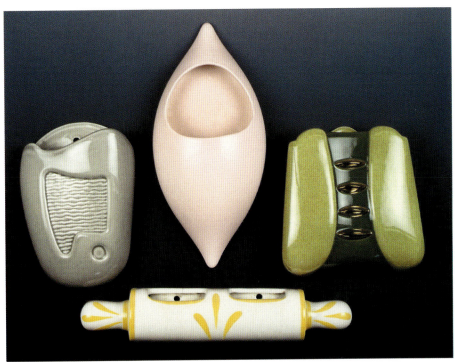

Knowles, Taylor & Knowles of California, ca. 1920s or 1930s. 7.25" wall pocket (and head vase), hand-incised KTK / F24 / 417. *Surry collection.* $40–50

Jervis Pottery (Oyster Bay, New York), ca. 1908–1912. 6.25" x 6" x 2.75" wall pocket, hand-incised seahorse motifs, hand-incised mark. *Grant collection.* $3000–3500. This motif shows the influence of Frederick Hurten Rhead (who also designed for Weller and then Roseville before going briefly to New York); it may have been designed by him.

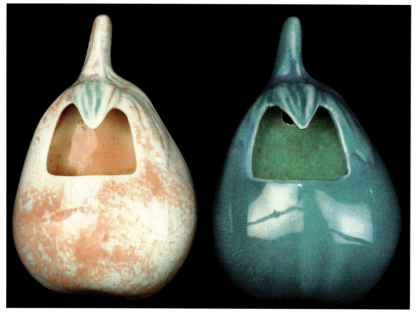

Lenox (Trenton, New Jersey), ca. 1930s. 7" t. x 8" wall pocket, green wreath LENOX logo / MADE IN U.S.A. (shape 2135; see Morin 74). *Gracyalny collection.* $350–450

Knowles, Taylor & Knowles of California (Santa Clara, California), ca. 1920s or 1930s. Pair, 6.25" wall pockets, pears. *Surry collection.* $25–35 (each). Left example hand-incised K T-K / California / 140 / 8; right example hand-incised K T & K / Calif. / 140. Although Lehner says the firm operated only during 1923 (page 238), the Chinese Modern style of many examples indicates some production in the 1930s.

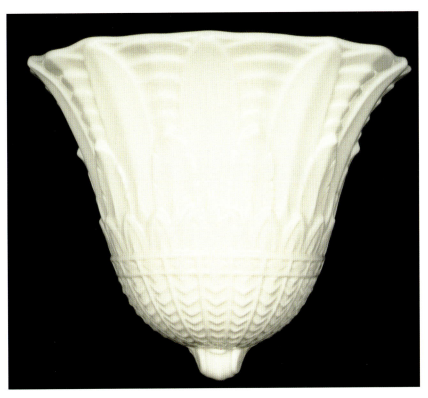

Lenox, ca. 1930s. 7.25" t. x 8.5" wall pocket, green wreath LENOX logo / MADE IN U.S.A., shape number unknown. *Gracyalny collection.* $350–450

Lenox, ca. 1980s. 10" x 8.5" wall pocket, irises, green wreath LENOX logo with ® symbol / MADE IN U.S.A., shape number unknown. *Surry collection.* $200–250

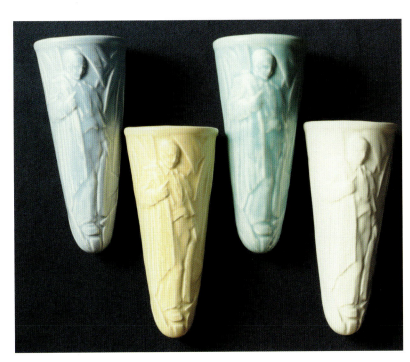

Nelson McCoy Pottery (Roseville, Ohio), ca. 1940. Four 7.25" wall pockets 101, Mexican man, unmarked. *Lindberg collection.* $75–100 (each)

McCoy, ca. 1942. Four 6" wall pockets WP 1, small lily with bud, die-impressed NM monogram / USA. *Lindberg collection.* $85–100 (each)

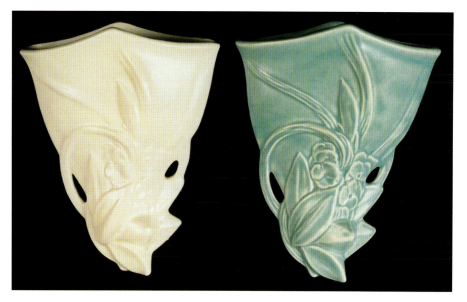

McCoy, ca. 1942. Two 8" wall pockets WP 2, fancy lily with blossoms, die-impressed McCoy. *Lindberg collection.* $250–300 (each)

McCoy, ca. 1942. 8" wall pocket WP 3, lady with bonnet, molded (raised relief) McCoy, probably repainted. *Lindberg collection.* $100–125

McCoy, ca. 1942. Four 7.75" wall pockets WP Z, large lily with bud, each with die-impressed NM monogram / USA. *Lindberg collection.* $225–275 (each)

McCoy, ca. 1942. Four 8" wall pockets WP 3, lady with bonnet, molded (raised relief) McCoy. *Lindberg collection.* $100–125 (each). *Caution:* A recent reproduction of this shape is known, measuring about 7.5" tall and made in several solid colors (without cold-painted details).

McCoy, ca. 1942. 8.5" wall pocket WP 4, lady harlequin, die-impressed McCoy. *Lindberg collection.* $125–175

McCoy, ca. 1942. 6" x 6.75" wall pocket 417, butterfly, die-impressed NM monogram. *Surry collection.* $275–350

McCoy, early 1940s. Two 7.25" wall pockets WP 7, leaves and berries, unmarked. *Lindberg collection.* $175–225 (each). *Caution:* A recent reproduction of this shape is known, in a somewhat smaller size, about 6.5" tall. The reproduction has a raised-relief (molded) McCoy mark; the original design was never marked.

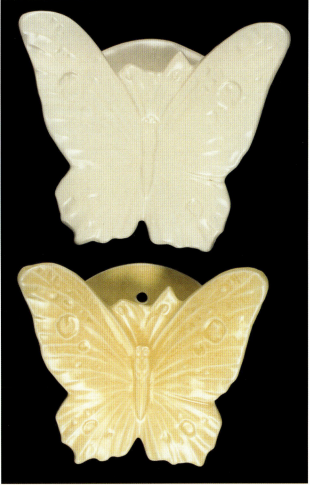

McCoy, ca. 1942. Two 6" wall pockets 417, butterfly, each die-impressed NM monogram. *Lindberg collection.* $275–350 (each)

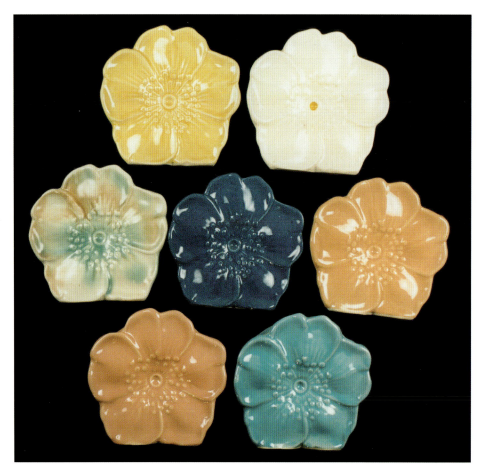

McCoy, ca. 1945. Seven 6" wall pockets WP 5, poppy, unmarked. *Lindberg collection.* $45–65 (each)

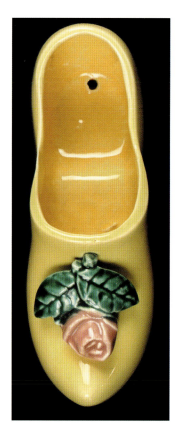

McCoy, ca. 1947. 7.5" wall pocket 23, Dutch shoe with rose, molded (raised relief) McCoy. *Lindberg collection.* $50–65. This shape is usually seen as a planter (without the hanging hole).

McCoy *Blossom Time*, ca. 1947. Three 7.5" wall pockets 708, molded (raised relief) McCoy. *Lindberg collection.* $100–125 (each)

McCoy, ca. 1948. Three 7.5" wall pockets 709, lily, molded (raised relief) McCoy / Made in USA. *Lindberg collection.* $100–125 (each)

McCoy, ca. 1949. Three 6.75" wall pockets 710, bird and daisy, molded (raised relief) McCoy. *Lindberg collection.* $75–100. This shape can also be used as a vase. It is difficult to find with the bird intact. *Caution:* A recent reproduction of this shape is known, with a bird of a slightly different shape, and standing about 6" tall. The reproduction is not marked McCoy.

McCoy, ca. 1940s. Three 6.75" wall pockets 5 W, maple leaves and berries, die-impressed McCoy. *Lindberg collection.* $70–90 (each). This shape was also made as a "windproof" ashtray (without the hanging hole).

McCoy, ca. 1940s. 9" wall pocket, woodpeckers, molded (raised relief) McCoy / USA. *Courtesy of Jeff Koehler.* $6500–7500. This rare shape saw only a limited production. In July 2002, this example was sold at auction by Jeff Koehler Real Estate and Auction Company (Zanesville, Ohio) for $7150 (including a 10% buyer premium).

McCoy, ca. 1940s. 9" wall pocket, geese, molded (raised relief) McCoy / USA. *Courtesy of Jeff Koehler.* $8500–9500. This rare shape saw only a limited production. In July 2002, this example was sold at auction by Jeff Koehler Real Estate and Auction Company (Zanesville, Ohio) for $9075 (including a 10% buyer premium).

McCoy, ca. 1950. Three 8" wall pockets 724, birdbath, molded (raised relief) McCoy. *Lindberg collection.* $125–175 (each). This shape is difficult to find with the bird intact.

McCoy, ca. 1952. Three 7.75" wall pockets 718, cuckoo clock, molded (raised relief) McCoy. *Lindberg collection.* $175–225 (each). The cuckoo clocks are often missing one or both weights, and the bird is often damaged.

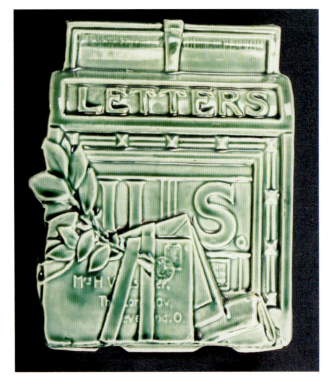

McCoy, ca. 1951. 6.75" wall pocket 729, mailbox, molded (raised relief) McCoy / USA (on base). *Lindberg collection.* $100–150. This shape can also be used as a vase. *Caution:* A recent reproduction of this shape is known, in a somewhat smaller size, about 6.25" to 6.5" tall. The original piece was made only in the glossy green glaze shown here.

McCoy, ca. 1952. Three 7.75" wall pockets 718, cuckoo clock, molded (raised relief) McCoy. *Lindberg collection.* $175–225 (each)

McCoy, ca. 1953. 7.25" wall pocket WP 6, apple, unmarked; 7.5" wall pocket WP 10, orange, cold-painted, die-impressed U. *Lindberg collection.* $75–100, $100–125

McCoy, ca. 1953. Two 7.25" wall pockets WP 9, bananas, left example die-impressed 5, other unmarked. *Lindberg collection.* $100–125 (each). Minor differences in decoration are typical of McCoy wall pockets.

McCoy, ca. 1953. Two 7.25" wall pockets WP 7, pear, unmarked. *Lindberg collection.* $75–100 (standard coloring), $125–150 (unusual white coloring)

McCoy, ca. 1953. Two 8.25" wall pockets WP 11, lovebirds on trivet, die-impressed McCoy / USA. *Lindberg collection.* $100–125 (each)

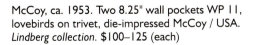

McCoy, ca. 1953. 8.25" wall pocket WP 12, owls on trivet, molded (raised relief) McCoy / USA. *Lindberg collection.* $100–125

McCoy, ca. 1956. Four 7.5" wall pockets WP 15, fan, molded (raised relief) McCoy / USA. *Lindberg collection.* $100–125 (each)

McCoy, ca. 1955. Four 8.75" wall pockets WP 14, parasol, molded (raised relief) McCoy / USA. *Lindberg collection.* $100–125 (each)

McCoy, ca. 1953. Three 8.5" wall pockets WP 13, iron on trivet, molded (raised relief) McCoy / USA. *Lindberg collection.* $100–125 (each)

McCoy *Sunburst Gold*, ca. 1957. 7.25" x 8.5" wall pocket WP 15, fan; 8.75" x 6" wall pocket WP 14, parasol—both with molded (raised relief) McCoy / USA, gilt round inkstamp reading 24K GOLD. *Surry collection.* $125–175 (each)

McCoy, ca. 1956. 9.25" wall pocket WP 16, bellows, non-production glaze, molded (raised relief) McCoy / USA. *Lindberg collection.* $275–350

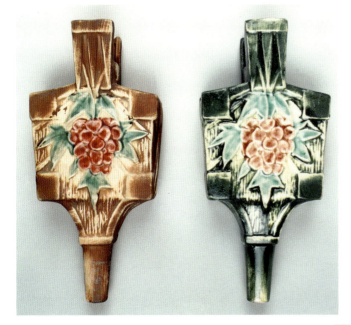

McCoy, ca. 1956. Two 9.25" wall pockets WP 16, bellows, each with molded (raised relief) McCoy / USA. *Surry collection.* $125–175 (each)

McCoy, ca. 1956. Three 7.5" wall pockets WP 18, basket weave, white example unmarked, others with molded (raised relief) McCoy. *Lindberg collection.* $85–100 (each)

McCoy, ca. 1956. Two 4.75" x 6.5" wall pockets WP 19, urn, molded (raised relief) McCoy / USA. *Lindberg collection*. $50–75 (each). This shape can also be used as a vase.

McCoy (Mt. Clemens era), ca. 1980s. Four 9.25" wall pockets 146, unmarked. *Lindberg collection*. $35–50 (each)

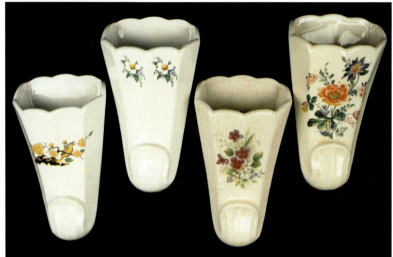

McCoy, ca. 1957. Four 10.25" wall pockets, violin, molded (raised relief) McCoy / USA. *Lindberg collection*. $125–150 (each)

McCoy (Mt. Clemens era), ca. 1980s. Four 9.25" wall pockets 146, unmarked. *Lindberg collection*. $35–50 (each)

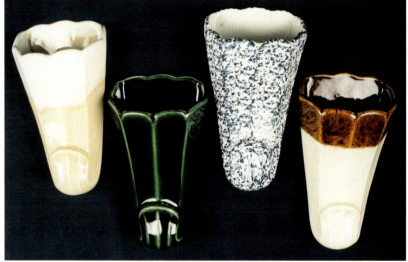

Marblehead, ca. 1920s. Four 5" x 4.25" wall pockets, die-impressed galleon logo—one (upper right) also with oval paper label. *Grant collection.* $450–550 (each)

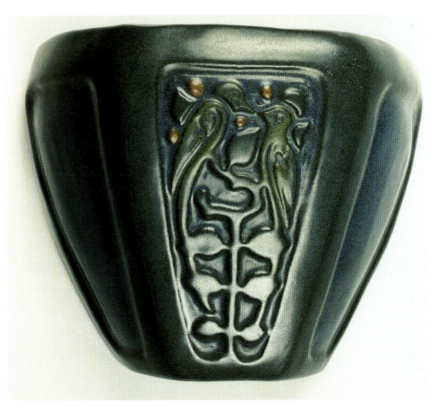

Marblehead, ca. 1910–1920. 5.5" x 7" wall pocket, molded design of birds in fruit tree, die-impressed galleon logo, hand-incised decorator initials (illegible). *Grant collection.* $1800–2200. In this example, the berries were colored red, against a blue background, adding a little more value than this shape commands in a solid color. Marblehead collectors prefer examples with hand-incised (instead of molded) decorations; vases with hand-incised decorated often command values around $10,000 (or more).

Marblehead, ca. 1910–1920. *Top:* 5" x 5.25" wall pocket, oval paper label; 4.5" x 5.5" wall pocket, oval paper label. *Bottom:* 4.75" x 5" wall pocket, unmarked; 4.75" x 5" wall pocket, die-impressed galleon logo. *Grant collection.* $600–700 (each)

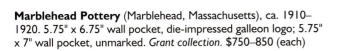

Marblehead Pottery (Marblehead, Massachusetts), ca. 1910–1920. 5.75" x 6.75" wall pocket, die-impressed galleon logo; 5.75" x 7" wall pocket, unmarked. *Grant collection.* $750–850 (each)

Monterey Art Pottery (Monterey, California), ca. late 1940s. Pair, 6.5" x 8.5" wall pockets, cornucopia, hand-incised MONTEREY / Art Pottery (script), brown inkstamp MONTEREY, CALIF. *Surry collection.* $50–60 (each, or $125–150 as a set).

Morton, ca. 1940s. 7" x 6" wall pocket, flowerpot and trellis, unmarked. *Grant collection.* $30–40. According to Marvin and Joy Gibson, this shape was attributed to Morton by Doris and Burdell Hall (see Gibson, Book I, pages 249–250). The piece can also be used as a vase.

Morton Pottery Co. (Morton, Illinois), ca. 1930s. 6" corner wall pocket, unmarked; 9" corner wall pocket, unmarked. *Surry collection.* $50–60, $75–100. According to Marvin and Joy Gibson, these shapes were attributed to Morton by Doris and Burdell Hall (see Gibson, Book I, page 249; and Gibson, Book II, pages 234–235).

Morton, ca. 1950s. 7.25" wall pocket, bird, unmarked. *Yonis collection.* $20–30. According to Marvin and Joy Gibson, this shape was attributed to Morton by Doris and Burdell Hall (see Gibson, Book I, pages 249 and 253–254). The piece can also be used as a planter.

Morton, ca. 1950s. 7.5" wall pocket, owl and crescent moon, unmarked. *Yonis collection.* $60–75. According to Marvin and Joy Gibson, this shape was attributed to Morton by Doris and Burdell Hall (see Gibson, Book I, pages 249 and 255–256). The piece can also be used as a vase.

Muncie Pottery (Muncie, Indiana), ca. late 1920s to 1930s. 8.5" wall pocket, hand-incised I; 9" wall pocket, hand-incised 3-I; 8.5" wall pocket, unmarked. *Grant collection.* $250–300, $275–350, $250–300. The middle example can be used as a freestanding vase.

Muncie, ca. late 1920s to 1930s. 6.5" wall pocket, hand-incised I. *Surry collection.* $200–250

Mountainside Art Pottery (Mountainside, New Jersey), ca. 1930s. 8" wall pocket, hand-incised MP (conjoined) monogram. *Surry collection.* $600–800

Newcomb College Pottery (New Orleans, Louisiana), 1910. 9.5" wall pocket, narcissus decoration, die-impressed and blue inkstamp NC monogram, die-impressed JM monogram (of potter Joseph Meyer), blue ink D.M.3 (date code for 1910), blue hand-painted initials AFS (of artist Anna Frances Simpson). *Grant collection.* $8,000–10,000. Although Newcomb Pottery wall pockets are rare, two more examples can be found in the *Journal of the American Art Pottery Association,* September–October 1999, page 9; and in Nancy E. Green and Jessie Poesch, *Arthur Wesley Dow and American Arts and Crafts* (New York: American Federation of Arts, and Abrams, 1999), page 144. In the fall of 2002, an early decorated glossy example was sold by ragoarts.com for about $10,000.

Niloak Pottery (Benton, Arkansas), ca. 1930s and 1940s. Two 6.5" wall pockets, handmade, attributed to Niloak, unmarked. *Grant collection.* $500–600 (each). Niloak's *Mission Swirl* wall pockets are not known to be marked, but their glaze is distinctive and several shapes are documented in Gifford.

Nicodemus *Ferro-Stone* Ceramics (Columbus, Ohio), ca. 1940s to 1990. 9.5" wall pocket, green, *courtesy of JoAnn and Bill Harrison*; 9" wall pocket, brown, *courtesy of Chester Sturm.* $350–450, $500–600

Niloak (attribution), ca. 1940s. 6.75" wall pocket, pinecones, molded shape, buff clay, unmarked. *Grant collection.* $75–100. This shape does not appear in Gifford, so its attribution to Niloak is only tentative.

George Ohr (or Biloxi Art Pottery, Biloxi, Mississippi), ca. 1883–1918. 4" wall pocket, unmarked. *Grant collection.* $3250–3750. Identified as George Ohr by David Rago, of www.ragoarts.com.

J.B. Owens Pottery (Zanesville, Ohio) *Utopian*, *Matt Utopian,* and *Venetian*, ca. 1902–1903. *Utopian* 5.75" wall pocket, underglaze slip decoration, unmarked, ca. 1902; *Utopian* 10" wall pocket, underglaze slip decoration, unmarked, ca. 1902; *Matt Utopian* 7.25" wall pocket, slip decoration, die-impressed shape number (illegible—possibly 812), TS monogram (of artist Tot Steele), ca. 1902; *Venetian* 5.75" wall pocket, metallic gold, unmarked, ca. 1903. *Grant collection.* $400–500, $600–700, $750–900, $200–250. These bamboo-figural shapes can be used as vases.

Overbeck Pottery (Cambridge City, Indiana), ca. 1920s to 1940s. 4.5" wall pocket, "grotesque" caricature of Southern belle, hand-incised OBK monogram. *Grant collection.* $2000–2500

Owens *Corona*, ca. 1902. 9.75" wall pocket, attributed to Owens, unmarked. *Grant collection.* $3500–4500. The torch held by this winged Liberty figure functions as a small vase. This design is closely related to an Owens kerosene lamp base illustrated in Hahn, page 41.

Attributed to Owens (*Utopian,* ca. 1905). 6.5" wall pocket, underglaze slip decoration, unmarked. *Grant collection.* $850–1000. Very little contemporary documentation of Owens' products is known. Comparable underglaze slip-decorated wares were made by Cambridge, Roseville, and Weller.

Owens Matt Green and *Utopian,* ca. 1905. Three 8" x 5" x 4.5" wall pockets, all die-impressed 700 (script)—one example (middle) with underglaze slip decoration. *Grant collection.* $700–800, $1200–1500, $700–800. Researchers have not distinguished Owens' Matt Green from the other four matte green Owens lines: *Aqua Verdi, Corona Green, Rustic,* and *Sylvan Green.* For a later Brush look-alike, see Sanford, Book I, page 131.

Owens Creamware (ca. 1905) and Matt Green lines (ca. 1905). Three 9.75" x 9.25" wall pockets, cornucopia with ribbon and bow, all die-impressed 704 (script)—one example (middle) also die-impressed OWENSART. *Grant collection.* $850–1000, $750–850, $850–1000

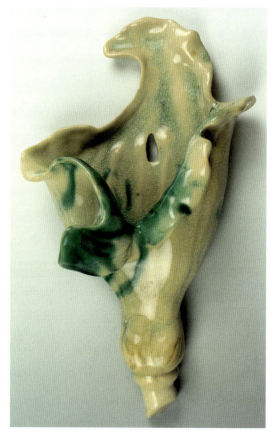

Owens *Majolica,* ca. 1905. 15.75" x 9.25" x 6" wall pocket, lily, shape 703, unmarked. *Grant collection.* $1200–1500. This design appears in a February 1905 Owens advertisement—reprinted in Hahn (page 32). According to the factory, the shape was only "one of the fifteen new wall ornaments for cut flowers." Most (if not all) Owens wall pocket designs were introduced that year.

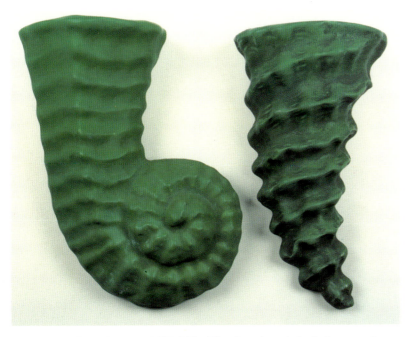

Owens Matt Green lines, ca. 1905. 9.5" x 7" wall pocket, shell, die-impressed 708 (script) and OWENSART; 9.75" x 5.25" wall pocket, conical shell, die-impressed OWENSART. *Grant collection.* $700–800, $550–650. For a Brush McCoy look-alike based on the Owens conical shell, see page 11.

Attributed to Owens, ca. 1905. 10" wall pocket, unmarked; 9.5" wall pocket, unmarked. *Grant collection.* $300–400 (each). These ribbed wall pockets may instead have been made by Roseville; if an attribution to Roseville could be properly documented, their value would probably be 50% higher (or more).

Owens *Corona* (left) and Matt Green lines (right), ca. 1905. Two 10.5" x 5.75" wall pockets, Chinese sage, one (left) die-impressed 709 (script). *Grant collection.* $850–1000 (each)

Permian Pottery (Frederick, Oklahoma), ca. late 1940s. 3.75" t. wall pocket, treble clef musical staff with lettering OES (Order of Eastern Star) and personalized "Bessie B. Harris / W.G.M. (Worthy Grand Matron) / 1949–50," foil label in shape of Oklahoma. *Private collection.* $50–60. There is no mention of this concern in Lehner or Bess.

55

Peters & Reed Pottery (or **Zane Pottery**) *Moss Aztec* (Zanesville, Ohio), ca. 1913 or later. 10" wall pocket (or cemetery vase), die-impressed Ferrell (script). *Johnson collection.* $175–225. Many Peters and Reed lines were made for years (or even decades); no published documentation specifies which shapes were the earliest in a given line. The dates cited here are approximate.

Peters & Reed *Moss Aztec*, ca. 1913 or later. 8.25" wall pocket; 9.5" wall pocket; and 8.5" wall pocket—all unmarked. *Grant collection.* $225–275, $250–300, $125–175

Peters & Reed *Moss Aztec*, ca. 1913 or later. 9.25" wall pocket, die-impressed Ferrel (script). *Surry collection.* $225–275

Peters and Reed *Maroon*, ca. 1920s. 8.5" wall pocket, unmarked. *Grant collection.* $125–175

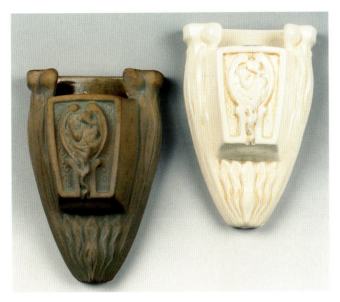

Peters & Reed *Moss Aztec* and *Ivory*, ca. 1913 or later. Two 9.25" wall pockets, unmarked—*Moss Aztec* (left) and *Ivory* (right). *Grant collection.* $225–275 (each)

Peters & Reed *Pereco*, *Ozane Ware*, and *Egyptian*, ca. mid-1920s. *Pereco* 8" wall pocket; *Ozane Ware* 7.75" wall pocket, Egyptian shape; *Egyptian* 8" wall pocket, semigloss green—all unmarked. *Grant collection.* $150–200, $150–200, $250–300

Peters & Reed *Wilse Blue*, ca. 1921. Two 8.5" wall pockets, one (left) decorated, both unmarked. *Grant collection.* $125–175, $100–150

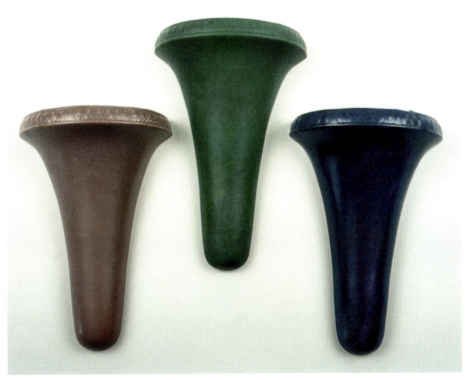

Peters & Reed *Persian Ware*, ca. mid-1920s; and *Matt Green*, ca. 1920. Three 8" wall pockets—Persian Ware (left and right) and Matt Green (middle), all unmarked. *Grant collection.* $150–200 (each)

Peters & Reed *Decorated Ivory,* ca. mid-1920s. 6" wall pocket; 7.5" wall pocket; 6" wall pocket; and 9.25" wall pocket—all unmarked except far right example, which has rectangular ZANE WARE inkstamp and blue hand-painted notations reading "special sample / #200 Glaze — O-G-Decorating / Chilcote" (script). Note: O-G is an abbreviation for overglaze. *Grant collection.* $275–350, $200–250, $150–200, $375–450 (or $275–350 without hand-painted notations)

Peters & Reed *Mirror Black,* ca. 1926; and *Victoria Ware,* ca. mid-1920s. Mirror Black 6" wall pocket, unmarked; Mirror Black 10.5" wall pocket, unmarked; and Victoria Ware 6" wall pocket, unmarked. *Grant collection.* $65–85, $100–125, $65–85

Peters & Reed *Florentine,* ca. mid-1920s. 8" wall pocket, rectangular ZANE WARE inkstamp. *Grant collection.* $250–300

Peters & Reed *Marbleized,* ca. late 1920s. 7.25" wall pocket, unmarked. *Grant collection.* $250–300. This "bird house" shape can also be used as a vase.

Peters & Reed *Mirror Black,* ca. 1926; and *Marbleized,* ca. late 1920s. Two 7.25" wall pockets, unmarked—Mirror Black and Marbleized. *Grant collection.* $175–225, $250–300

Pewabic Pottery (Detroit, Michigan), ca. 1920s or 1930s. 10" x 8.75" x 7.75" wall pocket, flowerpot, die-impressed logo reading PEWABIC / DETROIT. *Grant collection.* $3500–4000

Peters & Reed *Marbleized,* ca. late 1920s. 7.75" wall pocket; 7" x 6" wall pocket—both unmarked. *Grant collection.* $175–225, $250–300

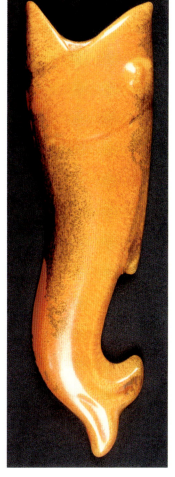

Pfaltzgraff Pottery (York, Pennsylvania), ca. late 1930s or 1940s. 11" wall pocket, fish, die-impressed logo of keystone reading YORK / P and 268, crayon notation 268. *Mark Bassett Antiques, Lakewood, OH.* $150–200

Pigeon Forge Pottery (Pigeon Forge, Tennessee), ca. 1970s to 1990s. Two 3.75" wall pockets, pitchers, both with black inkstamp marks The / Pigeon Forge / Pottery / Pigeon Forge / Tenn. *Surry collection.* $25–35 (each). This pottery closed in 2000, and values are currently on the increase.

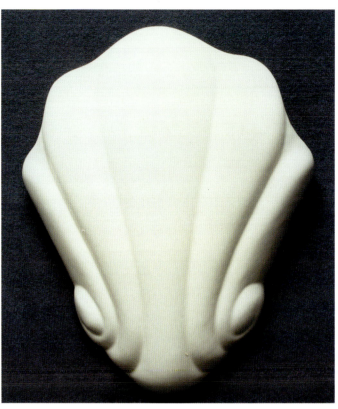

Red Wing, ca. 1946. 8" x 6.5" wall pocket 1254, shell, Eggshell Ivory, die-impressed RED WING / U.S.A. / 1254. *Surry collection.* $100–125

Red Wing Potteries (Red Wing, Minnesota), ca. 1929. 9" wall pocket 190, lilies, Light Green, blue inkstamp logo, die-impressed 190. *Surry collection.* $125–150

Red Wing, ca. 1955. 13.5" wall pocket, violin, Fleck Nile Blue, die-impressed RED WING / USA / M-1484. *Surry collection.* $60–75

Red Wing, ca. 1956. 7.5" x 12.25" wall pocket, Cinnamon, die-impressed RED WING / U.S.A. / M-1517. *Surry collection.* $75–100

Robinson Ransbottom *Luxor*, ca. 1926. 6.75" wall pocket, unmarked. *Grant collection.* $75–100

Robinson Ransbottom Pottery (Roseville, Ohio) *Luxor,* ca. 1926. 8.25" wall pocket, bird in grape vine, glossy green interior, unmarked. *Surry collection.* $85–125

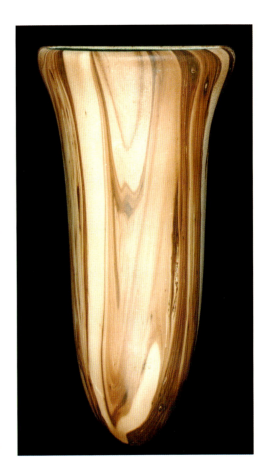

Rocky Mountain Pottery (Loveland, Colorado), ca. 1970s or 1980s. 8.75" wall pocket, rectangular black instamp reading MADE IN U.S.A. / BY / ROCKY MOUNTAIN / POTTERY. *Surry collection.* $45–60

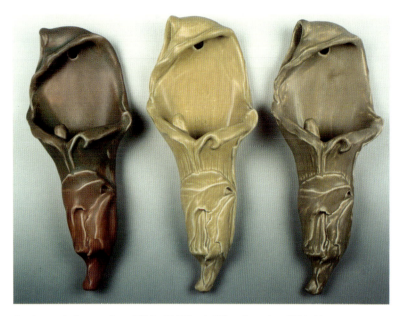

Rookwood, designed ca. 1904. 15.25" x 6.25" wall pocket 1036, lilies, introduced ca. 1904, dated XVIII (1918), and die-impressed P for Soft Porcelain body; XXII (1922); and XXII (1922). *Grant collection.* $1200–1500 (each)

Rookwood Pottery (Cincinnati, Ohio), *Modeled Mat*, designed ca. 1903. 16.5" x 9.25" x 4.75" wall pocket 625Z, fern fronds, hand modeled, dated III (1903). *Grant collection.* $2750–3250

Rookwood *Modeled Mat*, designed ca. 1903. 12.75" x 6.75" x 3" wall pocket 677Z, water lilies, hand modeled by Anna Maria Valentien (hand-incised A.M.V.), dated III (1903). *Grant collection.* $3000–3500

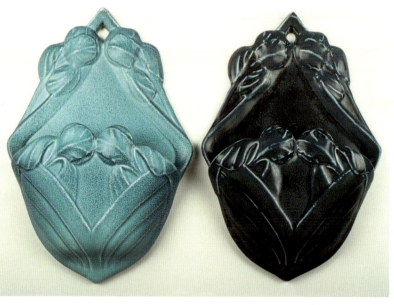

Rookwood, designed ca. 1905. Two 13" x 9" wall pockets 1083, irises, dated XVII (1917); and XX (1920). *Grant collection.* $2000–2500 (each)

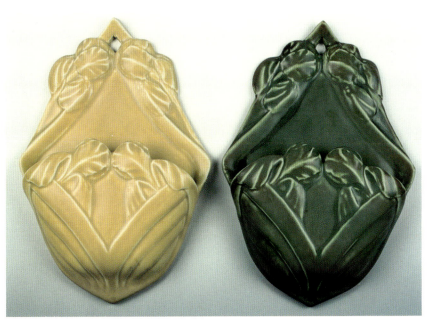

Rookwood, designed ca. 1905. Two 13" x 9" wall pockets 1083, irises, dated XXI (1921); and XXIV (1924). *Grant collection.* $2000–2500 (each)

Rookwood, designed ca. 1905. 12.5" x 5.25" wall pocket 1090? (indistinct mark), thistles, dated V (1905). *Grant collection.* $1800–2200

Rookwood, designed ca. 1905. 13" x 9" wall pocket 1083, irises, dated XXIV (1924). *Grant collection.* $2000–2500

Rookwood, designed ca. 1905. 15.5" x 8.375" wall pocket 251Z, buckeye, dated V (1905). *Surry collection.* $2000–2500

Rookwood, designed ca. 1908. Three 7.75" x 6" wall pockets 1389, foliage, dated XVI (1916); XXI (1921); and XXIV (1924). *Grant collection.* $600–800 (each)

Rookwood, designed ca. 1908. 11.75" wall pocket, marked 1392 [which appears in Peck, Vol. 2, as a 1908 Kataro Shirayamadani (KS) design involving fern fronds), hand-incised geometrical motif, dated XI (1911); and 11.5" wall pocket 1395, peacock feathers, designed by KS, dated XX (1920). *Grant collection.* $500–700, $600–800

Rookwood, designed ca. 1908. 6.5" x 6" wall pocket 1391, leaves and closed tulips, dated XIII (1913) (top); XXI (1921); and XXIV (1924). *Grant collection.* $500–700 (each)

Rookwood, designed ca. 1908. 11.25" wall pocket 1397, lilies, designed by KS, dated XIX (1919). *Courtesy of Cincinnati Art Galleries.* $450–550

Rookwood, designed ca. 1908. Two 11.25" wall pockets 1397, lilies, dated XXI (1921); and XVIII (1918), and die-impressed P for Soft Porcelain body. *Grant collection.* $450–550 (each)

Rookwood, designed ca. 1908. Three 8.5" wall pockets 1636, locust. *Grant collection.* $1500–2000 (each). The example at left is dated XVII (1917) and die-impressed P; the other two are dated XXII (1922).

Rookwood, designed ca. 1908. Three 8.5" wall pockets 1636, locust, designed by KS, two dated XVII (1917), and die-impressed P for Soft Porcelain body; and one (right) dated XXII (1922). *Grant collection.* $1500–2000 (each)

Rookwood, designed ca. 1908. 8.5" wall pocket 1636, locust, dated XX (1920). *Scally collection.* $1500–2000

Rookwood, designed ca. 1911. Five 7.75" wall pockets 2008, leaves, dated XIV (1914); XXII (1922); XXVIII (1928); XXV (1925); and XXII (1922). *Grant collection.* $300–400 (each)

Rookwood, designed ca. 1913. Four 9.5" wall pockets 2107, leaves and flowers, dated XV (1915); XXI (1921); XXIII (1923); and XXIV (1924). *Grant collection.* $350–450 (each). This design appears to have been derived from shape 2008.

Rookwood, designed ca. 1915. 12" x 6.25" wall pocket 2277, satyr and wisteria, designed by "Williams," dated XV (1915). *Grant collection.* $3000–4000

Rookwood, designed ca. 1915. 11.5" x 6.25" wall pocket 2276, satyr and grape vine, designed by "Williams" (first name unknown), dated XVI (1916), hand-incised X but no discernible factory flaw. *Grant collection.* $3000–4000. When a Rookwood piece is marked as a second, but there is no obvious factory defect, values are not generally affected. Although Roseville and Weller also marked some items with a hand-painted or die-impressed "X," *only* Rookwood Pottery used that mark to mean "factory second."

Rookwood, designed ca. 1915. 14" x 7.75" wall pocket 2278, squirrel and oak branch, designed by "Williams," dated XV (1915). *Grant collection.* $3000–4000

Rookwood, designed ca. 1915. 13" x 6.75" wall pocket 2279, rook and grape vine, designed by "Williams," dated XVI (1916). *Grant collection*. $3000–4000

Rookwood, designed ca. 1926. *Top:* 6" wall pocket 2965, incised lines, designed by KS, dated XXVII (1927); 6.375" wall pocket 2957, geometrical design, designed by KS, dated XXVI (1926). *Middle:* 6" wall pocket 2965, dated XXVII (1927); 6.75" x 3.75" wall pocket 2956, rectangular, designed by KS, dated XXVI (1926); 7.5" wall pocket 2958, designed by KS, dated XXX (1930). *Bottom:* 6" wall pocket 2965, dated XXVI (1926); 7" wall pocket 2954, geometrical design, designed by KS, dated XXVI (1926), hand-incised X, no discernible factory flaw. *Grant collection.* Top: $200–300 (each). *Middle:* $200–300 (each). *Bottom:* $200–300, $300–400

Rookwood, designed ca. 1926. *Top:* Three 7.75" wall pockets 2940, ridged body, geometrical design at tip, designed by KS, dated XXVI (1926); XXVIII (1928); and XXVIII (1928). *Bottom:* Three 7.5" wall pockets 2941, geometrical design, designed by KS, dated XXVIII (1928); XXVI (1926); and XXVI (1926). *Grant collection.* $200–300 (each). Because pink matte glazes are relatively common on such forms, these examples may be valued near the low end of the range.

Rosemeade Pottery (or Wahpeton Pottery, Wahpeton, North Dakota), ca. 1940s or 1950s. 4.5" wall pocket, leaves, unmarked. *Surry collection.* $75–100. Although the Wahpeton Pottery called their artware line *Rosemeade* and marked items that way, virtually everyone today calls the pottery "Rosemeade."

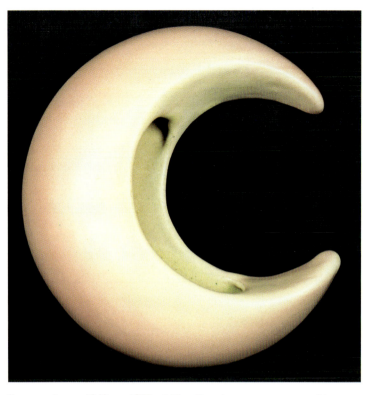

Rosemeade, ca. 1940s or 1950s. 4.5" wall pocket, crescent moon, blue inkstamp (script). *Surry collection*. $50–75. The rare 6.25" size of this shape is valued at $250–300.

Roseville *Matt Green,* ca. 1905–1916. 11" wall pocket, shape 328; 10" wall pocket, shape 327; 12" wall pocket, shape 1204. *Johnson collection*. $550–650, $2500–3000 (indistinct mold), $450–550 (crisp mold). No factory mark. For a *Creamware (Traced and Decorated)* version of shape 328, see *Introducing Roseville Pottery*, page 10.

Roseville *Matt Green,* ca. 1905. 10.25" wall pocket, shape 325, papoose. *Grant collection*. $4500–5000. No factory mark.

Roseville Pottery (Zanesville, Ohio) *Matt Green,* ca. 1905. 9" wall pocket, shape 324, nude witch on broomstick, with crescent moon. *Hoppe collection*. $4000–4500. No factory mark. The lines *Chloron, Egypto,* and *Matt Green* were all introduced in 1905. Instead of being unmarked, some examples of Roseville's rare ca. 1905 shapes may bear a Rozane Egypto wafer or a Chloron inkstamp. (For an example, see page 72.)

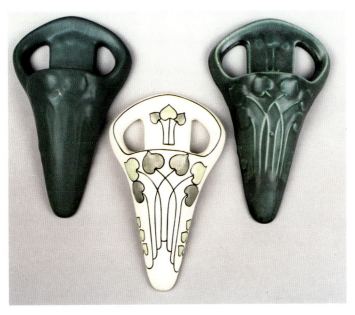

Roseville *Matt Green* and *Creamware (Traced and Decorated)*, ca. 1905–1916. Three 10" wall pockets, shape 326. *Johnson collection*. $350–400 (indistinct mold), $450–550, $400–500. No factory mark. Because these lines were made for more than a decade, individual examples are difficult to date precisely.

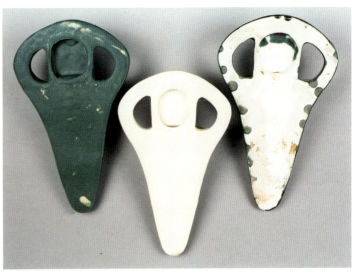

Another View of the *Matt Green* and *Creamware Wall Pockets*. Some collectors believe that differences in finishing the back of a Roseville wall pocket can be used to date specific examples. This subject warrants further research.

Roseville *Matt Green*, ca. 1905–1916. 10" wall pocket, shape 327. *Grant collection*. $3000–3500. No factory mark. Collectors describe a thickly applied matte green glaze with irregularly "veins" or color variations in its texture as being "organic." When such variations occur in an early Roseville piece, the term "Egypto glaze" is sometimes used, even when an Egypto wafer is not present.

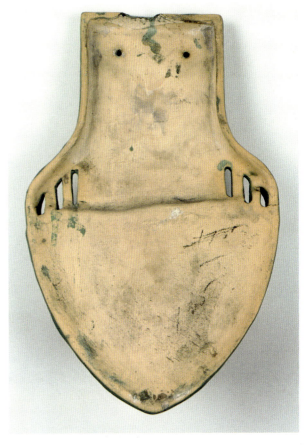

Another View of *Matt Green* Wall Pocket. Particularly when found on a rare shape like this, chips and short cracks (or firing lines) on the back surface of a wall pocket have little effect on value.

Roseville *Matt Green* and *Old Ivory (Tinted)*, ca. 1916. Four 10" wall pockets, shape 1204. *Johnson collection.* $400–500. No factory mark. Some Roseville *Matt Green* and *Old Ivory (Tinted)* wall pockets are marked only with a die-impressed shape number. The third example is *Old Ivory*—without any tinting in another color.

Roseville *Old Ivory (Tinted)*, ca. 1916. Four 15" wall pockets, shape 1202. *Johnson collection.* $600–700 (each). Because of its indistinct details, the example at the far right may be more accurately valued at $500–600.

Roseville *Antique Matt Green;* and *Matt Green*, ca. 1905–1916. *Matt Green* 10.5" wall pocket, shape number unknown (probably either 1210 or 1211); *Matt Green* 11" wall pocket, shape 329; *Antique Matt Green* 10" wall pocket, shape 1209. *Hoppe collection.* $550–650 (organic glaze), $1200–1500, $1500–1800. No factory mark. As shown here, *Matt Green* glazes can have considerable variety in color and texture. The middle and right shapes are rare.

Roseville *Early Carnelian*, ca. 1915. 12" wall pocket, shape number unknown (probably either 1210 or 1211). *Johnson collection.* $550–650. No factory mark. Roseville's *Early Carnelian* glaze can be difficult to distinguish from *Antique Matt Green*. For an example in the latter glaze, see page 74.

Roseville *Creamware (Decorated)*, ca. 1910–1916. 13" wall pocket, shape 335, hand-painted floral decoration; 3.75" hanging match holder, shape number unknown, hand-painted floral decoration, hand-incised shape number 9. *Grant collection.* $2000–2500, $1200–1500. No factory mark.

Roseville *Matt Green*, ca. 1905–1916. 13" wall pocket, shape 335; 11.5" wall pocket, shape 330. *Johnson collection.* $2000–2500, $1800–2200. No factory mark. Organic (or "Egypto") glazes.

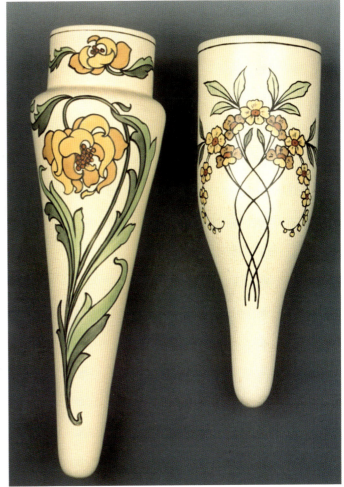

Roseville *Creamware (Persian)* and *Creamware (Traced and Decorated)*, ca. 1905–1916. 11" wall pocket, shape 330, hand-painted poppy; 10.75" wall pocket, molded phlox motif, traced and hand decorated. *Hoppe collection.* $2000–2500, $550–650. No factory mark.

Roseville *Creamware (Persian)*, ca. 1905–1916. 14" wall pocket, shape 334; 12" cemetery vase, shape 2. *Johnson collection.* $2000–2500, $1800–2200. No factory mark. The cemetery vase could be used as a wall pocket or pushed into the ground at a gravesite.

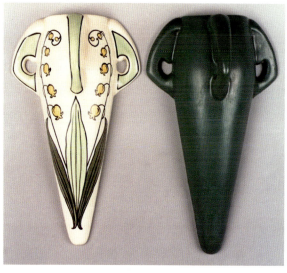

Roseville *Creamware (Persian)* and *Matt Green*, ca. 1905–1916. Two 11" wall pockets, shape 331. *Johnson collection.* $850–1000, $750–850. No factory mark. As shown here, a decorated Roseville *Creamware* wall pocket is usually worth a bit more than a *Matt Green* example with no variations in glaze color or texture.

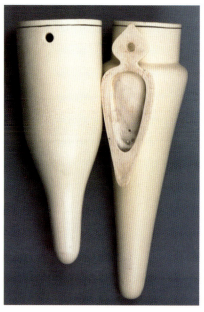

Obverse of *Creamware (Persian)* Pieces. *Left:* 12" cemetery vase. *Right:* 14" wall pocket. For a view showing the decorations, see page 71.

Roseville *Creamware (Persian)*, ca. 1905–1916. 11" wall pocket. *Grant collection.* $1500–1800 (or more). No factory mark. Rare shape, related to shape 331 but made without the applied handle in front nor a hanging hole in back. Collectors differ in opinion regarding this unusual example: it may be an otherwise undocumented shape, or it may represent a factory manufacturing error. In either case, it should be judged as more valuable than the standard production version.

Roseville *Egypto*, ca. 1905. 8.5" wall pocket, shape 332, fan with children and grape vine, Rozane Egypto wafer. *Hoppe photograph.* $3000–3500. *Egypto* pieces are marked with a ceramic Rozane Egypto wafer. Other examples of this shape may be unmarked or may bear a Chloron inkstamp. (See the comments on page 68.)

Roseville *Matt Green,* ca. 1905. 12" wall pocket, shape 333, woman holding vase. *Hoppe collection.* $3000–3500. No factory mark.

Roseville *Creamware (Traced and Decorated),* ca. 1905–1916. 18" corner wall pocket, shape 336; 17.5" wall pocket, shape 338. *Johnson collection.* $3000–3500, $1200–1500. No factory mark.

Roseville *Matt Green,* ca. 1905–1916. 18" corner wall pocket, shape 336. *Hoppe photograph.* $3000–3500. No factory mark. Organic (or "Egypto") glaze.

Roseville *Creamware (Landscape),* ca. 1910–1916. 2.75" x 3.25" wall pocket (or match holder), shape number unknown. *Surry collection.* $850–1000 (as shown, with hairlines and chip; $1200–1500 if mint). The wall pockets and other items assigned Roseville shape numbers 337, 339–340, 359 and 363–443 (if indeed they were manufactured) have not been identified. (See *Introducing Roseville Pottery,* pages 82 and 172.)

Roseville *Antique Matt Green,* ca. 1916. 10" wall pocket, shape number unknown (probably either 1210 or 1211), unmarked; 12" x 6" wall pocket, shape 1208, unmarked; 13" wall pocket, unmarked, shape number unknown (probably either 1210 or 1211); 12" x 6" wall pocket, pencil shape number 1210 and "Antique / Green." *Grant collection.* $325–375, $650–750, $500–600, $400–500. No factory mark. Note the variations in coloring that can characterize *Antique Matt Green.* Research on Roseville shape numbers is an ongoing project. (For details, see www.MarkBassett.com.) Another example of the shape at far right bears a paper label with the shape number 1211 (see Mark Bassett, *Introducing Roseville Pottery,* page 41).

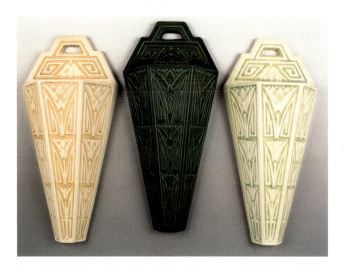

Roseville *Old Ivory (Tinted)* and *Matt Green,* ca. 1916. Three 14.5" wall pockets, shape 1201, unmarked. *Grant collection.* $600–700, $700–800, $600–700

Attributed to Roseville, ca. 1916. Two 12" wall pockets, attributed to Roseville (perhaps shape 1210 or 1211), white matte glaze with tracing and hand decoration, unmarked. *Grant collection.* $1000–1200 (or more, each). These wall pockets were said to originate in the collection of a former Roseville employee. Although the shape is not shown in factory records, its outline is identical to that of several documented Roseville wall pockets illustrated in this book. If their maker were properly authenticated, these examples could be worth more than the estimate shown. Any reader locating an example of this shape with a die-impressed shape number is asked to contact the author.

Roseville *Old Ivory (Tinted)* and *Matt Green,* ca. 1916. Three examples of shape 1203 (in two sizes): 12" wall pocket; 10" wall pocket; 12" wall pocket. *Johnson collection.* $350–450, $300–350, $350–450. No factory marks.

Roseville *Donatello,* ca. 1916. 10" wall pocket, shape 1212; 12" wall pocket, shape 1212. *Johnson collection.* $175–250, $275–350. Donatello usually has no factory mark. Some examples have a round die-impressed DONATELLO mark, which also reads R. P. CO. Examples made in 1923 or later may have a blue Rv inkstamp. (See Mark Bassett, *Understanding Roseville Pottery,* for more information about dating *Donatello* and other lines.) *Caution:* Items marked "R.R.P. Co., Roseville, O." were made by the Robinson Ransbottom Pottery Co., not by Roseville Pottery.

Roseville *Creamware (Tourist),* ca. 1916. 10" x 5" wall pocket, shape 1209. *Grant collection.* $12,000–15,000. Very rare. No factory mark. This example is die-impressed 1209, but others may be unmarked.

Roseville *Old Ivory (Tinted)* and *Matt Green,* ca. 1916. Two 1205-7" wall pockets, each die-impressed 1205. *Hoppe collection.* $400–500 (each). No factory mark.

Roseville *Matt Green,* ca. 1916. 1206-5" wall pocket, die-impressed 1206; 7.25" wall pocket, attributed to Roseville, shape number unknown (perhaps 1207), unmarked. *Hoppe collection.* $400–500, $600–700. No factory mark.

Roseville *Cherub Cameo* (attribution), ca. 1916–1920. 9.75" wall pocket, shape number unknown (perhaps 1214), unmarked. *Grant collection.* $400–500. Roseville wall pocket shape number 1214, assigned between 1916 and 1920, has not been matched with the corresponding item. Compare the outline of this wall pocket to that of the *Mostique* wall pockets shown here. For more information on *Cherub Cameo*, see Mark Bassett, *Understanding Roseville Pottery*, pages 253–257, 260.

Roseville *Mostique,* ca. 1920. Two 10" wall pockets, shape number unknown, brown, unmarked. *Grant collection.* $400–500 (each)

Roseville *Rozane Line,* ca. 1920. Three 10" wall pockets, shape 1215. *Johnson collection.* $400–475, $350–400, $400–475. Usually unmarked. Examples made in 1923 or later may have a blue Rv inkstamp.

Roseville *Mostique,* ca. 1920. 10" wall pocket, shape number unknown (perhaps 1214), gray, unmarked. *Johnson collection.* $400–500. It is possible that shape number 1214 was assigned to two different wall pockets. Around 1920, Roseville vases in different lines sometimes shared the same shape number. (See *Bassett's Roseville Prices,* page 186–187.) Other factory errors are also known. For example, the pottery inadvertently skipped one hundred shape numbers in the hanging basket sequence—namely, those between shape numbers 362 (*Bleeding Heart*) and 463 (*Foxglove*), both introduced in 1940. Our moral: "to err is human…"

Roseville *Rozane Line*, ca. 1920. 10" wall pocket, shape 1215. *Grant collection.* $350–400. Usually unmarked. Examples made in 1923 or later may have a blue Rv inkstamp.

Roseville *Imperial (Textured)*, ca. 1921. 10" wall pocket, shape 1223; 7" wall pocket, shape 1221; 9" wall pocket, shape 1222. *Johnson collection.* $300–350, $275–325, $300–350. No factory mark.

Roseville *Mostique*, ca. 1921. 10" wall pocket, shape 1224; 12" wall pocket, shape 1224. *Johnson collection.* $350–400, $450–550. No factory mark. Examples made in 1923 or later may have a blue Rv inkstamp. *Note:* The original ca. 1916 *Mostique* designs did not include a wall pocket.

Roseville *Dogwood (Smooth)*, ca. 1920. 8.75" double wall pocket, shape number unknown; 10" wall pocket, shape 1220; 10.25" wall pocket, shape number unknown; 15" wall pocket, shape 1217. *Grant collection.* $450–500, $600–700, $350–450, $800–900. No factory mark. Roseville wall pockets 1218 and 1219, introduced about 1920, have not been identified; they were probably assigned to two of the *Dogwood (Smooth)* shapes illustrated here.

Roseville *Rosecraft*, ca. 1921–1925. Five 1225-10" wall pockets. *Johnson collection.* $225–275 (Burnt Orange), $200–250 (each, Azurine, Orchid, Yellow, Turquoise). Examples made between 1921 and 1923 have no factory marks. Examples made in 1924 or later have a blue Rv inkstamp.

Roseville *Corinthian*, ca. 1923. 8" wall pocket, shape 1232; 12" wall pocket, shape 1229; 10" wall pocket, shape 1228. *Johnson collection.* $275–350, $500–600, $300–400. Blue Rv inkstamp; some examples may be unmarked.

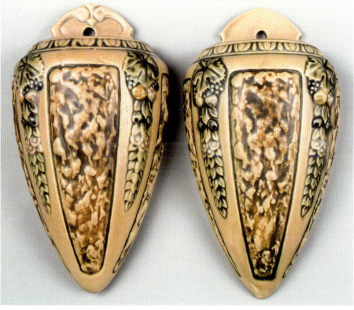

Roseville *Early Rosecraft* (or *Scottish Rose*), ca. 1922. 12" wall pocket, shape 1227; 11" wall pocket, shape 1226. *Johnson collection.* $500–600, $450–550. Usually no factory mark, but examples made in 1923 or later may have a blue Rv inkstamp.

Roseville *Florentine*, ca. 1924. Two 10" wall pockets, shape 1230. *Johnson collection.* $500–600, $300–350. Blue Rv inkstamp or unmarked. Note the unusual trim at the top of the example at the left.

Roseville *La Rose*, ca. 1924. 7" wall pocket, shape 1233; 11" wall pocket, shape 1235; 8" wall pocket, shape 1234. *Johnson collection.* $325–375, $450–550, $375–450. Blue Rv inkstamp or unmarked.

Roseville *Rosecraft*, ca. 1924–1925. Four 10" wall pockets, shape 1237. *Grant collection.* $250–300 (each, Azurine, Black, Yellow), $275–325 (Burnt Orange). Blue Rv inkstamp.

Roseville *Rosecraft*, ca. 1924–1925; and *Ivory*, ca. 1932. Four 9" wall pockets, shape 1236, in various *Rosecraft* glazes; one 9" wall pocket, shape 1236, in *Ivory*; and one (at bottom right) in a Trial Glaze blend of matt yellow and olive, unmarked. *Grant collection.* $225–275 (each, Azurine, Yellow, Black), $250–300 (Burnt Orange), $200–250 (*Ivory*), $600–700 (Trial Glaze). Blue Rv inkstamp. The *Ivory* wall pocket does not appear in the known factory pages; because this example has no factory mark, we know it was made between 1932 and 1935. Most Trial Glaze pieces have crayon glaze notations.

Roseville *Florentine*, ca. 1925 (right) and ca. 1936 (left). 1238-8" wall pocket, "Florentine Ivory" glaze, die-impressed factory marks; 8" wall pocket, shape 1238. *Johnson collection.* $350–450, $300–350. The "Florentine Ivory" glaze was introduced around 1935 (for the factory page, see Bomm 146). Since die-impressed factory marks (including the shape number and size) were introduced in 1936, we know that the example shown here (left) was made in 1936 or later.

Roseville *Florentine*, ca. 1925. 7" wall pocket, shape 1239; 12" wall pocket, shape 1231. *Johnson collection.* $200–250, $350–450. Blue Rv inkstamp or unmarked.

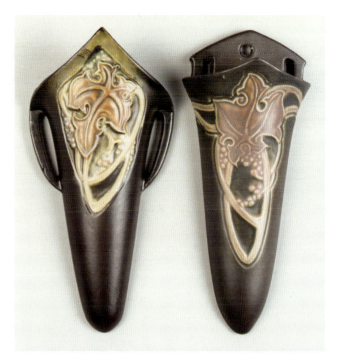

Roseville *Vintage,* ca. 1925. 8" wall pocket, shape 1241; 9" wall pocket, shape 1242. *Johnson collection.* $375–450, $500–600. Blue Rv inkstamp or unmarked.

Roseville *Hexagon,* ca. 1925. Three 8" wall pockets, shape 1240. *Grant collection.* $450–550 (brown), $600–700 (green), $1000–1200 (blue). Blue Rv inkstamp or unmarked.

Roseville *Panel,* ca. 1926. 9" wall pocket, shape 1244; two 9" wall pockets, shape 1243; 9" wall pocket, shape 1244. *Johnson collection.* $450–550, $500–600, $400–500, $375–450. Blue Rv inkstamp. Examples made in 1927 or later may have a paper label or may be unmarked.

Roseville *Carnelian (Drip)*, ca. 1926; and *Carnelian (Glazes)*, ca. 1928. Three 8" wall pockets, shape 1247. *Left and right: Carnelian (Drip). Middle: Carnelian (Glazes). Grant collection.* $350–450, $500–600, $350–450

Roseville *Dogwood (Textured)*; ca. 1926; and *Jonquil*, ca. 1930. 9" wall pocket, shape 1245; 8.5" wall pocket, shape 1268. *Johnson collection.* $350–450, $1000–1200. *Dogwood (Textured)* usually has a blue Rv inkstamp, but can be unmarked. *Jonquil* either has a paper label or is unmarked. *Caution:* A recent Chinese reproduction of the *Jonquil* wall pocket has a strongly curved rim and a background with less texture, in a blend of green and blue. It has raised marks reading Roseville (script).

Roseville *Carnelian (Drip)*, ca. 1926; and *Carnelian (Glazes)*, ca. 1928. Five 7" wall pockets, shape 1246. *Top: Carnelian (Drip). Bottom: Carnelian (Glazes). Grant collection.* $275–350 (each, top row), $550–650 (each, bottom row). *Carnelian (Drip)* items have a blue Rv inkstamp. *Carnelian (Glazes)* can have the same mark and/or a paper label.

Roseville *Carnelian (Drip)*, ca. 1926; and *Carnelian (Glazes)*, ca. 1928. Three 8" wall pockets, shape 1248. *Left and right: Carnelian (Drip). Middle: Carnelian (Glazes). Grant collection.* $300–400, $400–500, $300–400

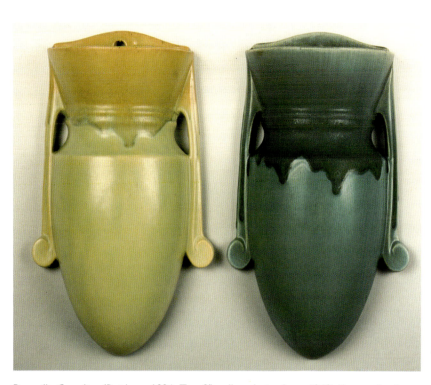

Roseville *Carnelian (Drip)*, ca. 1926. Two 9" wall pockets, shape 1249. *Grant collection.* $400–500 (each). In June 2002 a rare *Carnelian (Glazes)* version of this shape sold on *www.ebay.com* for just over $2200.

Roseville *Carnelian (Drip)* and *Carnelian (Glazes)*, ca. 1927. Four 8" wall pockets, shape 1251. *Left:* Carnelian (Drip). *Right:* Carnelian (Glazes). *Grant collection.* $275–350 each (left), $450–550 each (right)

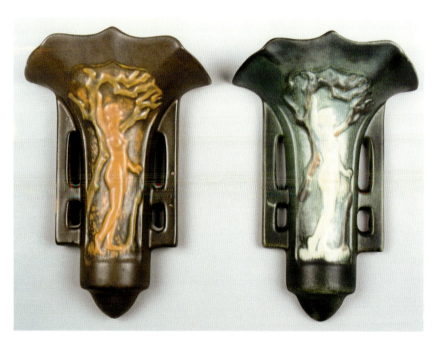

Roseville *Panel*, ca. 1927. Two 7" wall pockets, shape 1250. *Johnson collection.* $800–1000, $1000–1200. Blue Rv inkstamp. Examples made in 1927 or later may have a paper label or may be unmarked. *Caution:* A recent American reproduction of this wall pocket is known. One color combination is glazed in white with aqua on the figure. The other is brown, with a tan figure (instead of reddish brown) and dark brown tree and leaves. These fakes have a blue inkstamp using a variation on the Rv monogram in which the "v" is located lower than in the original. (For a photograph of the white and aqua fake and the fake mark, see Mark Bassett, *Understanding Roseville Pottery,* page 296.)

Roseville *Carnelian (Drip)* and *Carnelian (Glazes)*, ca. 1927. Four 8" wall pockets, shape 1252. *Top:* Carnelian (Drip). *Bottom:* Carnelian (Glazes). *Grant collection.* $275–350 each (top), $450–550 each (bottom)

Roseville *Carnelian (Drip)* and *Carnelian (Glazes)*, ca. 1927. Three 1253-8" wall pockets, shape 1253. *Left and right:* Carnelian (Drip). *Middle:* Carnelian (Glazes). *Grant collection.* $300–400, $450–550, $300–400

Roseville *Lombardy*, ca. 1928. 8" wall pocket, shape 1256; two 8" wall pockets, shape 1257; 8" wall pocket, shape 1256. *Johnson collection.* $300–350, $250–300, $250–300, $300–350. Paper label or unmarked.

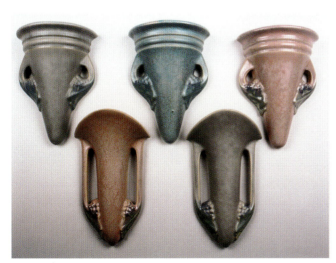

Roseville *Tuscany*, ca. 1928. *Top:* three 7" wall pockets, shape 1254. *Bottom:* two 8" wall pockets, shape 1255. *Johnson collection. Top:* $200–250, $375–450, $250–300. *Bottom:* $300–400, $275–350. Paper labels or unmarked.

Roseville *Dahlrose*, ca. 1928–1929. 8" wall pocket, shape 1258; 10" wall pocket, shape 1259. *Johnson collection.* $300–350, $375–450. Paper label or unmarked.

83

Roseville *Imperial (Glazes)*, ca. 1930. 6" wall pocket, shape 1262; 6" wall pocket, shape 1264. *Grant collection*. $850–1000, $650–750. Paper label or unmarked. These shapes were not made in *Earlam* glazes.

Roseville *Savona*, ca. 1929. Four 8" wall pockets, shape 1260. *Grant collection*. $650–750 (each). Paper labels or unmarked.

Roseville *Futura*, ca. 1929. Two 1261-8" wall pockets, shape 1261. *Johnson collection*. $1800–2200 (Trial Glaze), $600–700. Paper label or unmarked. The example at left has trial glaze notations reading "#T76–41" and a black paper label.

Roseville *Earlam*, ca. 1930. 6" wall pocket, shape 1263. *Johnson collection*. $700–800. Paper label or unmarked.

Roseville *Earlam* and *Imperial (Glazes)*, both ca. 1930. Three 6" wall pockets, shape 1263. *Top: Earlam* (mottled brown and blue), *Earlam* (green and blue). *Bottom: Imperial (Glazes). Grant collection. Top:* $850–1000, $1000–1200. *Bottom:* $850–1000. Paper label or unmarked. Distinguishing *Earlam* from *Imperial (Glazes)* wall pockets can require familiarity with the various glazes that define these lines.

Roseville *Blackberry*, ca. 1932; and *Vista*, ca. 1920. *Blackberry* 8" wall pocket, shape 1267; *Vista* 9" wall pocket, shape 1216. *Grant collection.* $1500–1800, $1200–1500. *Blackberry* either has a foil label or is unmarked. *Vista* is unmarked, or may have a blue inkstamp shape number.

Roseville *Baneda*, ca. 1932. Two 8" wall pockets, shape 1269. *Grant collection.* $3500–4000 (pink), $3750–4250 (green). Foil label, or unmarked.

Roseville *Ferella*, ca. 1930. Two 6.5" wall pockets, shape 1266. *Johnson collection.* $1750–2000 (brown), $2000–2500 (red). Paper label or unmarked.

Roseville *Cherry Blossom,* ca. 1933; and *Sunflower,* ca. 1930. *Top:* Two *Cherry Blossom* 8" wall pockets, shape 1270. *Bottom:* *Sunflower* 7" wall pocket, shape 1265. *Grant collection.* $1500–1800 (pink *Cherry Blossom,* at left), $1000–1200 (brown *Cherry Blossom,* at right), $1500–2000 (*Sunflower*). These patterns can have paper labels or can be unmarked.

Roseville *Luffa,* ca. 1934. Two 8" wall pockets, shape 1272. *Grant collection.* $650–750 (brown), $750–850 (green). Foil label or unmarked. *Caution:* A recent Chinese reproduction of this wall pocket is known, with raised marks reading Roseville (script) and 8-1/2. The reproduction has differently shaped leaves and a solid-color background. For photographs of the reproduction and its fake mark, see Mark Bassett, *Introducing Roseville Pottery,* page 284.

Roseville *Wisteria,* ca. 1933. Two 8.5" wall pockets, shape 1271. *Grant collection.* $1500–1750 (brown), $1750–2000 (blue). Foil labels or unmarked. Examples with a more prominent section of blue in the background are valued somewhat higher.

Roseville *Pine Cone,* ca. 1935; and *Ivory,* ca. 1939. Three *Pine Cone* 1273-8" wall pockets; *Ivory* 1273-8" wall pocket. *Grant collection.* $450–550 (green), $600–700 (brown), $750–850 (blue), $300–350 (*Ivory*). Early *Pine Cone* examples have foil labels or are unmarked; examples made in 1936 or later, including *Ivory,* have die-impressed marks.

86

Roseville *Velmoss*, ca. 1935. Three 8" wall pockets, shape 1274. *Grant collection*. $3000–3500 (blue), $2500–2800 (rose), $2200–2500 (green). Paper or foil labels or unmarked. If an example were made in 1936 or later, it might have die-impressed factory marks.

Roseville *Orian*, ca. 1935. Three 8" wall pockets, shape 1276. *Johnson collection*. $1000–1200 (each). Foil label or unmarked. The blue and red colorings are in greater demand than tan.

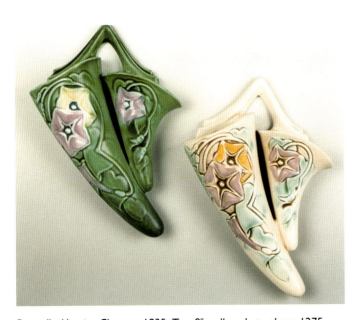

Roseville *Morning Glory*, ca. 1935. Two 8" wall pockets, shape 1275. *Grant collection*. $1500–1800 (green), $1200–1500 (white). Foil label or unmarked. Examples made in 1936 or later have die-impressed factory marks.

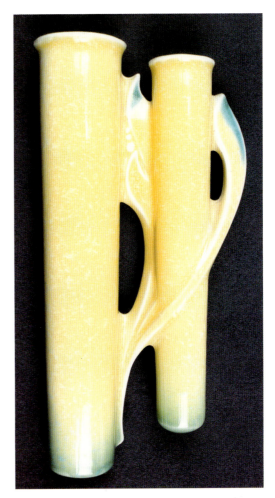

Roseville *Orian*, ca. 1935. 8" wall pocket, shape 1276. *Surry collection*. $1200–1500. Foil label or unmarked. The yellow coloring seems to be the most rare.

Roseville *Primrose*, ca. 1936. Three 1277-8" wall pockets. *Johnson collection.* $800–900 (blue), $700–800 (tan or pink). Die-impressed factory marks.

Roseville *Moss*, ca. 1936. Three 8" wall pockets, shape 1278. *Johnson collection.* $750–850 (each). Foil label or unmarked. Examples made in 1936 or later have die-impressed factory marks.

Roseville *Moss*, ca. 1936. 4" wall pocket, shape 1279. *Johnson collection.* $1200–1500

Roseville *Moss*, ca. 1936. Two 4" wall pockets, shape 1279. *Johnson collection.* $1200–1500 (each)

Roseville *Thorn Apple*, ca. 1937. Three 1280-8" wall pockets. *Johnson collection.* $700–800 (each). Die-impressed factory marks.

Roseville *Thorn Apple*, ca. 1937. Two 356 wall pockets, 4" each. *Johnson collection*. $1200–1500 (each). Die-impressed factory marks. Although collectors view this shape as a wall pocket, Roseville categorized it as a hanging basket. (That is why the shape number is *not* in the 1200s with the other 1937–1938 wall pockets.)

Roseville *Poppy*, ca. 1938. 1281-8" wall pocket. *Johnson collection*. $1000–1200. Die-impressed factory marks. If an example of this shape were made in 1939 or later, it would have raised-relief (molded) marks instead.

Roseville *Thorn Apple*, ca. 1937. 356 wall pocket, 4" each. *Grant collection*. $1200–1500. Die-impressed factory marks.

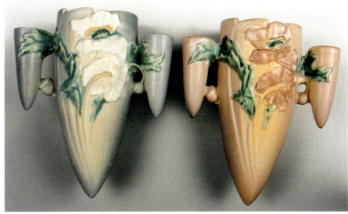

Roseville *Poppy*, ca. 1938. Two 1281-8" wall pockets. *Johnson collection*. $1000–1200 (each). Die-impressed factory marks. If an example of this shape were made in 1939 or later, it would have raised-relief (molded) marks instead.

Roseville *Fuchsia*, ca. 1938. Three 1282-8" wall pockets. *Johnson collection*. $1000–1200 (blue), $750–850 (brown or green). Die-impressed factory marks. *Caution:* A recent Chinese reproduction of this wall pocket has less texture in the background and more muted colors, especially on the leaves and flowers. It has raised marks reading Roseville (script) / 1282-8".

Roseville *Iris*, ca. 1939. Three 1284-8" wall pockets. *Johnson collection*. $750–850 (each). Die-impressed factory marks. Some examples may be unmarked or have very faint marks. *Caution:* Two recent Chinese reproductions of this wall pocket are known, each bearing raised (not die-impressed) marks reading Roseville (script) / 1284-8". The reproductions have a more evenly scalloped rim and differently shaped flowers.

Roseville *Pine Cone*, ca. 1938–1939. Three 1283-4" wall buckets. *Grant collection*. $1200–1400 (blue), $850–1000 (brown or green). Die-impressed factory marks. If an example of this shape were made in 1938, it would have a paper label instead (or would be unmarked).

Roseville *Cosmos*, ca. 1939. Three 1285-6" wall pockets. *Johnson collection*. $450–500 (blue or green), $375–450 (brown). Die-impressed factory marks. Some examples may be unmarked or have very faint marks.

Roseville *Cosmos*, ca. 1939. Three 1286-8" wall pockets. *Johnson collection.* $700–800 (blue or green), $600–700 (brown)

Roseville *White Rose*, ca. 1940. Three 1288-6" wall pockets. *Grant collection.* $300–350 (each). Raised-relief (molded) factory marks.

Roseville *Bleeding Heart*, ca. 1940. Three 1287-8" wall pockets. *Grant collection.* $700–800 (each). Raised-relief (molded) factory marks. *Caution:* A recent Chinese reproduction of this wall pocket has slightly different handles, wider leaves, and more pronounced stems and veins. Like the original, it has raised marks reading Roseville (script) and 1287-8".

Roseville *White Rose*, ca. 1940. Four 1289-8" wall pockets. *Grant collection.* $400–500 (each, but $700–800 for the unusually green example at bottom right). Raised-relief (molded) factory marks. *Caution:* A recent Chinese reproduction of this wall pocket has a wider flared shape and differently shaped buds. The detailing of the flowers and leaves is more crude. Like the original, it has raised marks reading Roseville (script) / 1289-8".

Roseville *Columbine*, ca. 1941. Three 1290-8" wall pockets. *Grant collection.* $700–800 (each). Raised-relief (molded) factory marks.

Roseville *Foxglove*, ca. 1942. Three 1292-8" wall pockets. *Johnson collection.* $375–450 (each). Raised-relief (molded) factory marks. *Caution:* A recent Chinese reproduction of this wall pocket has a different rim, simplified blossoms, and a solid-colored background. Like the original, it has raised marks reading Roseville (script) / 1292-8".

Roseville *Bushberry*, ca. 1941. Three 1291-8" wall pockets. *Johnson collection.* $450–550 (blue), $400–500 (green), $375–450 (brown)

Roseville *Peony*, ca. 1942. Three 1293-8" wall pockets. *Johnson collection.* $300–350 (each). Raised-relief (molded) marks. *Caution:* A recent Chinese reproduction of this wall pocket has a smooth background (not textured). Like the original, it has raised marks reading Roseville (script) / 8".

Roseville *Magnolia*, ca. 1943. Three 1294-8" wall pockets. *Johnson collection*. $300–400 (each). Raised-relief (molded) marks.

Roseville *Freesia*, ca. 1945. Three 1296-8" wall pockets. *Johnson collection*. $300–350 (each). Raised-relief (molded) factory marks. *Caution:* Two recent Chinese reproductions of this wall pocket are known, both (like the original) bearing raised marks reading Roseville (script) / 1292-8". One has a straight rim, the other rounded. The flowers on the reproductions are slightly different from those on the real Roseville pocket. The reproduction with the rounded rim has very little texture on the background, which is a solid color.

Roseville *Clematis*, ca. 1944. Three 1295-8" wall pockets. *Johnson collection*. $225–275 (each). Raised-relief (molded) factory marks.

Roseville *Zephyr Lily*, ca. 1946. Three 1297-8" wall pockets. *Johnson collection*. $275–350 (each). Raised-relief (molded) factory marks.

Roseville *Apple Blossom*, ca. 1949. Three 366-8" wall pockets. *Johnson collection*. $350–400 (each). Raised-relief (molded) factory marks.

Roseville *Wincraft*. Three 267-5" wall pockets. *Johnson collection*. $275–325 (each). Raised-relief (molded) factory marks.

Roseville *Snowberry*, ca. 1947. Three IWP-8" wall pockets. *Johnson collection*. $275–325 (each). Raised-relief (molded) factory marks.

Roseville *Wincraft*, ca. 1948. Three 266-5" wall pockets. *Johnson collection*. $250–300 (each). Raised-relief (molded) factory marks.

Roseville *Ming Tree*, ca. 1949. Four 566-8" wall pockets. *Johnson collection.* $375–450 (each, standard colors), $550–650 (with gold trim). Raised-relief (molded) marks.

Roseville *Bittersweet*, ca. 1951. Three 866-7" wall pockets. *Johnson collection.* $350–400 (green), $300–350 (yellow or gray). Raised-relief (molded) factory marks. *Caution:* A recent Chinese reproduction of this wall pocket has slightly different handles, wider leaves, and a glossy glaze. Like the original, it has raised marks reading Roseville (script) and 866-7".

Roseville *Silhouette*, ca. 1950. Four 766-8" wall pockets. *Johnson collection.* $225–275 (each). Raised-relief (molded) factory marks.

Roseville *Gardenia*, ca. 1950. Three 666-8" wall pockets. *Johnson collection.* $275–350 (each). Raised-relief (molded) factory marks.

Roseville *Mayfair*, ca. 1952. 1013-5" wall pocket. *Grant collection.* $1800–2200. Raised-relief (molded) marks. This rare shape does not appear in the known Roseville factory pages. In addition, this example has trial glaze notations. (Compare the glaze to the standard *Mayfair* glazes shown elsewhere.)

Roseville *Mayfair*, ca. 1952. Three 1014-8" corner wall pockets. *Grant collection.* $175–225 (each). Raised-relief (molded) marks.

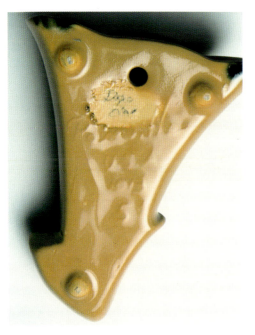

Obverse of *Mayfair* wall pocket.

Roseville *Lotus*, ca. 1952. Four L8-7" wall pockets. *Johnson collection.* $300–400 (each). Raised-relief (molded) marks, including the line name LOTUS.

Roseville *Pine Cone Modern*, ca. 1953. 466 triple wall pocket. *Schultz collection*. $700–800 (brown). Raised-relief (molded) factory marks; no size follows the shape number.

Roseville *Pine Cone Modern*, ca. 1953. Two 466 triple wall pockets. *Johnson collection*. $850–1000 (blue), $600–700 (green). Raised-relief (molded) factory marks; no size follows the shape number.

RumRill Pottery (Mt. Gilead, Ohio), ca. 1938–1941. 9.5" x 6.875" wall pocket, wishing well, die-impressed "i8" and "RumRill" (fancy lettering). *Mark Bassett Antiques, Lakewood, OH*. $50–75. This shape was derived from a vase design; although it is flat on the back, it too can be used as a vase.

Sebring Pottery (Sebring, Ohio), ca. 1929 to early 1930s. 7.25" wall pocket; 10" wall pocket; 7.25" wall pocket—all unmarked. *Bassett collection*. $100–125, $125–150, $100–125. These shapes were derived from vases of a similar design; they can function as vases, but are flat on the back.

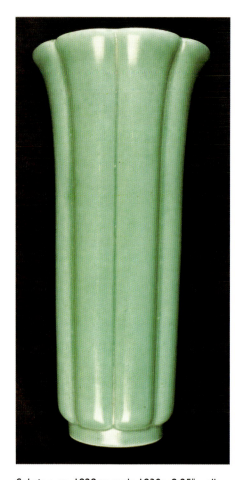

Sebring, ca. 1929 to early 1930s. 9.25" wall pocket, round paper label reading ART / CERAMIC / by / Sebring (script), with pencil notation 218 on label. *Bassett collection.* $75–100. Derived from a similar vase design and flat on the back, this wall pocket is not free standing.

S.E.G., ca. 1920s. Four 6" wall pockets. *Top:* Unmarked; paper label, black hand-painted S.E.G. and date 6-21, artist initials EG (Edith Guerrier). *Bottom:* Unmarked; black hand-painted date 12-23, artist initials CS. *Grant collection.* $300–400 (each)

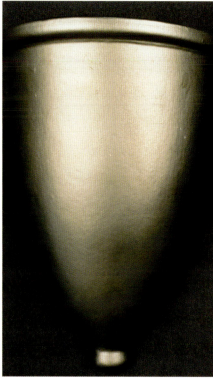

S.E.G. (that is, **Saturday Evening Girls,** or **Paul Revere Pottery,** Boston, Massachusetts), ca. 1920. 9" x 6.25" wall pocket, Paul Revere paper label. *Grant collection.* $450–550. In 1915 this pottery relocated to Brighton, Massachusetts.

S.E.G., 1927. 9" x 6.25" wall pocket, stylized decorated band, black hand-painted S.E.G. and date 10-27, artist monogram of Edith Brown. *Grant collection.* $2000–2500

Shawnee Pottery (Zanesville, Ohio), ca. late 1930s or 1940s. 6" wall pocket, attributed to Shawnee, die-impressed MADE IN USA. *Surry collection*. $25–35. This shape does not appear in Curran, so the attribution is tentative.

Shearwater, ca. late 1980s or 1990s. 7.25" wall pocket, die-impressed SHEARWATER / JA monogram / 01, hand-incised D / P. *Courtesy of Mike Nickel and Cindy Horvath*. $1500–2000

Shearwater Pottery (Ocean Springs, Mississippi), ca. late 1980s or 1990s. 7.5" wall pocket, die-impressed SHEARWATER / JA monogram / 39. *Surry collection*. $175–225

Spaulding China (Sebring, Ohio) *Royal Copley*, ca. 1940s or 1950s. Two 8.25" wall pockets, molded (raised relief) Royal Copley (script). *Surry collection*. $75–100 (each). The decorations are based on well-known paintings. Black inkstamp notations at the bottom right provide the source. *Left:* Constable / "The Cornfield" / Amsterdam Holland. *Right:* Constable / "Valley Farm" / Amsterdam Holland.

Stanford Pottery (Sebring, Ohio), ca. 1950s. 7.5" t. wall pocket, cup and saucer, hand-incised 223-B, molded (raised relief) Stanford, Sebring, O. logo (script) / die-impressed MADE IN / USA. *Surry collection.* $40–50

Strobl Pottery (Cincinnati, Ohio), ca. 1907. 10.5" x 9.5" wall pocket, die-impressed on top front J.H. STROBL / 908 DEPOT ST. *Seery photograph.* $1000–1200

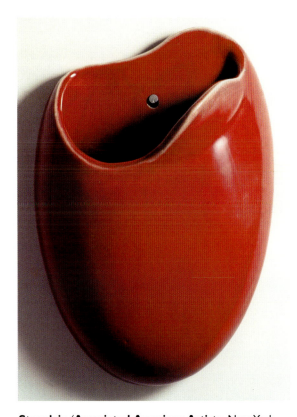

Strobl, ca. 1908. 14" x 5.75" wall pocket, die-impressed SP monogram and VIII (for 1908). *Seery photograph.* $1000–1200

Stonelain (**Associated American Artists**, New York, New York), ca. 1940s. 9.25" x 6.25" wall pocket, die-impressed logo and STONELAIN. *Photograph by Vera Kaufman, Buried Treasures/Vintage Vera (Manchester, NH).* $300–400

Strobl, ca. 1907-1910. 14" x 6.5" wall pocket, die-impressed SP monogram and 306. *Seery photograph.* $850-1000

Strobl, ca. 1907–1910. 15.25" x 6" wall pocket, die-impressed SP monogram and 258; 13.25" x 5.75" wall pocket, die-impressed STROBL and hand-incised 104. *Grant collection.* $1000–1200 (each)

Strobl, ca. 1907–1910. 13" x 6.25" wall pocket, die-impressed VII (for 1907), SP monogram and 255; 12.25" x 6.25" wall pocket, die-impressed 102 and STROBL; 13" x 6.5" wall pocket, unmarked. *Grant collection.* $850–1000, $750–850, $850–1000

Tamac Pottery (Perry, Oklahoma), ca. 1950s to early 1970s. Two 4.5" wall pockets, black inkstamp Tamac / PERRY, OKLA. / U.S.A. *Surry collection.* $60–75 (each)

Teco, ca. 1905–1920. 16" x 8.5" wall pocket, die-impressed 156 (script). *Grant collection.* $2750–3500. *Note:* Several different Teco designs were assigned the shape number 156.

Teco Pottery (or Gates Pottery, or American Terra Cotta, Terra Cotta, Illinois—near Crystal Lake), ca. 1905–1920. *Top:* 6.5" x 5.25" wall pocket, shape 439A, two die-impressed TECO marks. *Bottom:* 7" x 9.25" wall pocket, shape 82, two die-impressed TECO marks. *Grant collection.* $1000–1200 (each)

Teco, ca. 1905–1920. 16.75" wall pocket, shape 156A, two die-impressed TECO marks. *Grant collection.* $2750–3500

Teco, ca. 1905–1920, versus Haeger, ca. 1990s. Teco 14.5" x 7" wall pocket, shape 156B, three die-impressed TECO marks and 156, hand-incised B, ca. 1905–1920; Haeger 11" x 5.25" wall pocket, unmarked, ca. 1990s. *Grant collection.* $2000–2500, $75–100. The Haeger glaze used on the wall pocket shown at right is called Grueby Green.

Van Briggle Pottery (Colorado Springs, Colorado), ca. 1930s. Three 7.75" wall pockets, Mountain Craig Brown (left and right), and Mulberry (middle). *Grant collection.* $375–450, $250–300, $375–400. Van Briggle wall pockets made in earlier years are worth more than those made in the 1930s or later. For information on dating Van Briggle, see Sasicki and Fania.

Van Briggle, ca. 1940s or 1950s. 5" wall pocket; 10.5" wall pocket—both Ming Blue. *Grant collection.* $275–350, $325–375

Van Briggle, ca. 1930s. 8" wall pocket; 10.5" wall pocket. *Surry collection.* $375–450, $450–550. These examples were made with dark buff clay.

Van Briggle, ca. 1940s or 1950s. *Top:* Two 4.75" wall pockets, Persian Rose (left) and Ming Blue (right). *Bottom:* Two 7.25" wall pockets, Ming Blue (left) and Persian Rose (right). *Grant collection. Top:* $250–300, 200–250 (each). *Bottom:* $400–500, $500–600

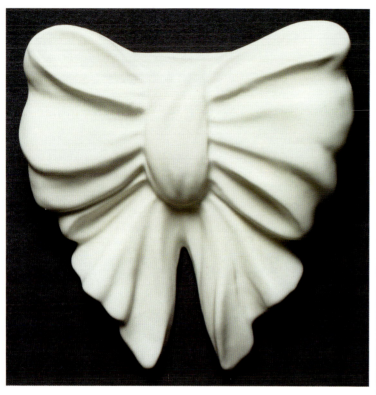

Van Briggle, ca. 1970s or 1980s. 9" x 8.75" wall pocket, bow. *Surry collection.* $150–200

Weller Pottery (Zanesville, Ohio) *Art Nouveau,* ca. 1904. 6.25" wall pocket, unmarked. *Grant collection.* $1200–1500

J.W. Walley (West Sterling, Massachusetts), ca. 1905–1919. 5.5" x 4.25" wall pocket; 6.25" x 4.5" wall pocket—both unmarked. *Grant collection.* $750–850 (each)

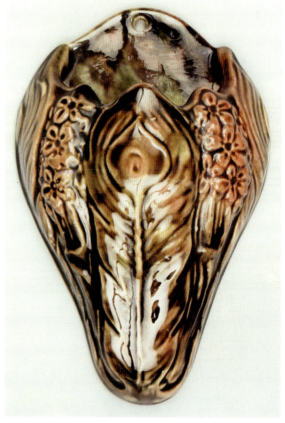

Weller *Majolica,* ca. 1904. 6.25" wall pocket, feather, unmarked. *Surry collection.* $700–800

Weller *Louwelsa (Matt)*, ca. 1905. 7.25" wall pocket, die-impressed WELLER. *Harris collection.* $1200–1500. In Sharon and Bob Huxford's Weller book (page 217), this example is assigned to the Weller line *Perfecto*. Additional research is needed.

Weller *Matt Green,* ca. 1905. 6" x 4" wall pocket, unmarked; 12.25" wall pocket, unmarked; 9" x 4.75" wall pocket, unmarked. *Grant collection.* $400–500, $650–750, $550–650. The middle shape was also produced as *Souevo*. All three examples have the paint-like green glazed bottom typical of much Weller *Matt Green. Caution:* This bottom finish is also found on some Roseville Pottery items.

Weller *Dickens Ware III,* ca. 1905. 4" x 4.25" wall pocket, die-impressed WELLER. *Grant collection.* $3250–3750. This grotesque figural wall pocket is quite rare; its value can only be approximated.

Weller *Souevo,* ca. 1907. 8" corner wall pocket; and 12.25" corner wall pocket—both unmarked. *Grant collection.* $450–550, $600–700

Weller *Souevo*, ca. 1907; *Matt Green*, ca. 1905; and *Bo Marblo*, ca. 1915. *Souevo* 13.75" wall pocket, unmarked; *Matt Green* 14.5" wall pocket, unmarked; *Bo Marblo* 13.75" wall pocket, die-impressed WELLER. Grant collection. $650–750, $600–700, $800–900

Weller *Souevo*, ca. 1907. 8.5" wall pocket; 6.25" wall pocket; and 8.75" wall pocket—all unmarked. Grant collection. $350–450, $200–250, $300–400

Weller *Souevo*, ca. 1907. 9.25" wall pocket; and 9.75" corner wall pocket—both unmarked. Grant collection. $350–450, $400–500

Weller *Burnt Wood*, ca. 1908; *Knifewood*, ca. 1921; and *Selma*, ca. 1923. *Top:* Two 5.5" wall pockets—*Burnt Wood*, unmarked (left); and *Selma*, black hand-painted 7 (right). *Bottom:* Three 8.25" wall pockets—*Burnt Wood*, unmarked (left); *Knifewood*, unmarked (middle); and *Selma*, die-impressed WELLER, black hand-painted 3 (right). Grant collection. Top: $200–250, $250–300. Bottom: $275–325, $375–450, $350–400

Weller *Burnt Wood*, ca. 1908. 5.5" wall pocket, daisies with unusual orange coloring, unmarked. *Grant collection.* $350–450

Weller *Ivory*, ca. 1910; and *Alvin*, ca. 1927. Two 6.75" wall pockets—one unmarked (left) and one with *Alvin* paper label (right). *Grant collection.* $850–1000, $750–850

Weller *Ivory*, ca. 1910. 11.75" x 5.75" wall pocket, die-impressed WELLER, chips, crazing. *Grant collection.* $200–250 (or $300–400 without damage)

Weller *Ivory*, ca. 1910. 8.75" wall pocket; 10.75" wall pocket; 10" wall pocket. *Grant collection.* $750–850, $850–1000, $750–850. These pockets are die-impressed WELLER (stylized lettering).

Weller *Roma*, ca. 1912. 6" wall pocket; 7" wall pocket—both die-impressed WELLER. *Grant collection.* $300–400, $400–500

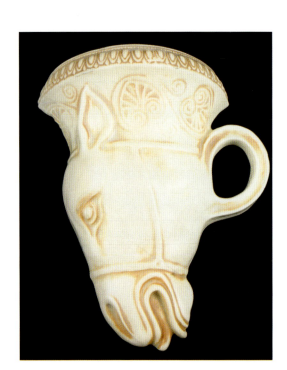

Weller *Ivory*, ca. 1910. 8" x 7.25" wall pocket, die-impressed WELLER (stylized lettering). *Grant collection.* $750–850

Weller *Roma*, ca. 1912. 8.5" x 6.75" wall pocket, unmarked. *Grant collection.* $1000–1200 (hairline, or $1400–1600 without damage). Note that the *Muskota*-type cupid figure was cast separately and attached by hand.

Weller *Ivory*, ca. 1910; *Arcola*, ca. 1920s; and Unknown Line, ca. 1920s. Two 8" wall pockets, unmarked, one *Ivory* (left) and the other an unknown line; *Arcola* 10.5" wall pocket, paper White Pillars Museum label. *Grant collection.* $150–225, $600–700, $125–175

Weller *Roma*, ca. 1912; and Unknown Maker. 8.25" x 3.75" wall pocket, die-impressed WELLER; 8" x 3.5" wall pocket, buff clay, unmarked. *Grant collection*. $150–200, $100–150. Weller is not known to have used the Rockingham-type spatter glaze seen at right. This smaller wall pocket may have been produced by another maker.

Weller *Roma*, ca. 1912. 5.25" wall pocket, unmarked; 7.75" wall pocket, die-impressed WELLER. *Grant collection*. $275–350, 350–450

Weller *Roma*, ca. 1912. 6.25" wall pocket, unmarked; 7.5" wall pocket, die-impressed WELLER, black hand-painted 14; 7" wall pocket, unmarked; 5.75" wall pocket, die-impressed WELLER. *Grant collection*. $250–300, $150–225, $200–250, $250–300. The far right example is also known in a brown matte *Flemish* glaze.

Weller *Bo Marblo*, ca. 1915. 14.75" wall pocket, hand-incised WELLER. *Grant collection*. $850–1000

Weller *Hudson, White and Decorated*, ca. 1917. 7.75" wall pocket, floral, unmarked; 10" wall pocket, raspberries; 13.75" wall pocket, floral; 9" wall pocket, bird and berries—die-impressed WELLER, unless otherwise noted. *Grant collection.* $600–800, $1000–1200, $1200–1500, $2000–2500. *Hudson* pieces featuring birds or other figures are more valuable than those decorated with flowers or fruit.

Weller *Florala*, ca. 1920. 10" wall pocket, unmarked. *Grant collection.* $300–400

Weller *Parian*, ca. 1920s. Three 8.25" wall pockets, unmarked, one (right) with paper White Pillars Museum label. *Grant collection.* $175–250 (each)

Weller *Florala*, ca. 1920; *Roma*, ca. 1912; and *Dupont*, ca. 1915. *Florala* 8.5" wall pocket, brown hand-painted 3; *Florala* 9.5" wall pocket, brown hand-painted 14; *Roma* 10.5" wall pocket, green hand-painted XL; *Roma* 10.5" wall pocket, green hand-painted RL; *Dupont* 8" wall pocket, unmarked. *Grant collection.* $250–300, $300–400, $250–300, $250–300, $250–300

Weller *Brighton*, ca. 1916. 14.75" x 8.75" wall pocket, unmarked. *Grant collection.* $850–1000. The owner of this wall pocket has added wires that facilitate safe hanging.

Weller *Flemish*, ca. 1917. 10.5" x 9.75" wall pocket, die-impressed WELLER. *Grant collection.* $2000–2500

Weller *Brighton*, ca. 1916. 11.75" x 5.75" wall pocket, unmarked. *Grant collection.* $850–1000. The owner of this wall pocket has added wires that facilitate safe hanging.

Weller *Flemish*, ca. 1917. 15" x 12.75" wall pocket, die-impressed WELLER. *Grant collection.* $2000–2500

Weller *Flemish*, ca. 1917; and *Wood Rose*, ca. 1925. *Top:* Two *Flemish* 6" wall pockets, fan shape, one (left) die-impressed WELLER; *Wood Rose* 6.75" wall pocket, die-impressed WELLER, black hand-painted 2X. *Bottom: Flemish* 8.75" wall pocket, die-impressed WELLER; *Wood Rose* 9.5" wall pocket, die-impressed WELLER, hand-incised 20-11, black hand-painted 39. *Grant collection. Top:* $275–350, $125–175, $275–350. *Bottom:* $400–500, $225–275

Weller *Wood Rose*, ca. 1925–1930s. *Top:* 5.25" x 6.5" wall pocket, unmarked; 6.5" x 7.5" wall pocket, unmarked. *Bottom:* 6.5" x 7.5" wall pocket, die-impressed WELLER and 84-3, brown hand-painted XII. *Grant collection. Top:* $125–150, $150–200. *Bottom:* $200–250

Weller *Wood Rose*, ca. 1930s. Two 6.5" wall pockets, unmarked. *Grant collection.* $125–175 (each). In 1925, the background colors (shown in another photograph) were matte brown and green; the straps were glazed to resemble metal. These pastel examples were probably made in the 1930s.

Weller *Woodcraft*, ca. 1917. 8.75" wall pocket, unmarked; 9" wall pocket, die-impressed WELLER; 11.25" wall pocket, unmarked; 7.75" wall pocket, unmarked. *Grant collection.* $750–850, $550–650, $550–650, $750–850

Weller *Woodcraft*, ca. 1917. 9.25" wall pocket; and 10.75" wall pocket—both die-impressed WELLER. *Grant collection.* $225–275, $300–400

Weller *Woodcraft*, ca. 1917; and Unknown Maker. Weller *Woodcraft* 9.25" wall pocket, unmarked; 8.5" wall pocket, pencil notation "Test #4." *Grant collection.* $150–225, NPD (pending documentation of maker). These two pieces differ significantly in size, weight, and finishing; the example on the right was probably derived from the *Woodcraft* shape.

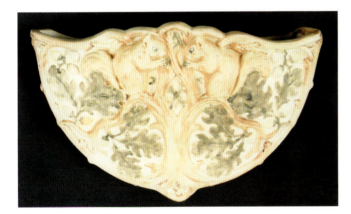

Weller *Woodcraft*, ca. 1917. 8.25" x 12.75" wall pocket, die-impressed WELLER. *Grant collection.* $2500–3000

Weller *Cloudburst*, ca. 1921; and *Lustre*, ca. 1922. *Cloudburst* 6.75" wall pocket; *Lustre* 7.25" wall pocket, worn glaze; *Cloudburst* 7.25" wall pocket—all unmarked. *Grant collection.* $250–300, $75–100 (or $125–175, in good condition), $250–300

Weller *Cloudburst,* ca. 1921; *Lavonia,* ca. 1927; and Unknown Line, ca. 1930s. Three 8.5" wall pockets. *Grant collection.* $250–300, $125–175, $250–300. One example is die-impressed WELLER (right); the others are unmarked.

Weller *Marengo,* ca. 1926. Four 7.5" wall pockets, unmarked. *Grant collection.* $125–175, worn (or $300–350 undamaged); $100–150 with white splotches through decoration (as shown, or $350–400 with design intact); $200–250, minor wear (or $350–400 undamaged); $300–350

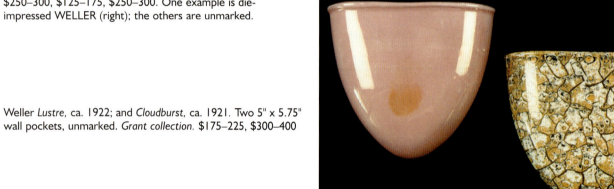

Weller *Lustre,* ca. 1922; and *Cloudburst,* ca. 1921. Two 5" x 5.75" wall pockets, unmarked. *Grant collection.* $175–225, $300–400

Weller *Lustre,* ca. 1922. Three 7" wall pockets—two unmarked, and one (right) with Weller Ware paper label. *Grant collection.* $125–175 (each)

Weller *Blue Ware,* ca. 1918; *Fairfield,* ca. 1916; and *Warwick,* ca. 1929. 10" wall pocket, unmarked; 8.25" wall pocket, die-impressed WELLER; 11.5" wall pocket, inkstamp "half kiln" Weller Pottery mark, black and silver foil "half kiln" label, blue hand-painted 11X. *Grant collection.* $275–350, $225–275, $250–300

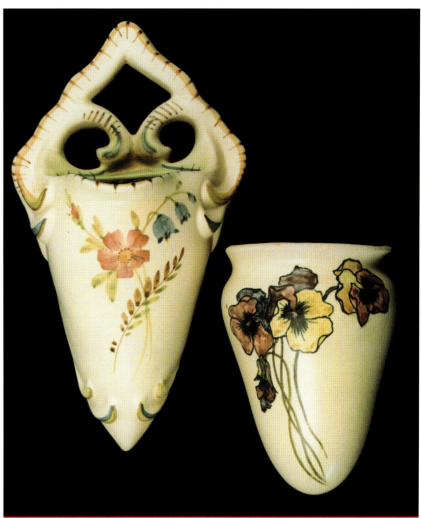

Weller *Bonito,* ca. 1932; and *Hudson (White and Decorated),* ca. 1920s. 10.5" wall pocket, die-impressed Weller Pottery (script); 6" wall pocket, die-impressed WELLER. *Grant collection.* $750–850, $1200–1400

Weller *Fruitone,* ca. 1919. Two 6" wall pockets, both die-impressed WELLER. *Grant collection.* $550–650 (each)

Weller *Blue Drapery,* ca. 1921; *Mirror Black,* ca. 1923; and *Unknown Lines,* ca. 1920s. Four 7.75" wall pockets, three being unmarked and one (far left) die-impressed WELLER. *Grant collection.* $125–175 (each)

Weller *Orris Ware*, ca. 1922. 7.5" wall pocket, unmarked. *Grant collection*. $175–225

Weller *Tivoli*, ca. 1920s. 8" wall pocket, hand-painted 12, hand-incised 14. *Grant collection*. $225–275. Compare this design to the 9.5" Weller *Euclid* wall pockets.

Weller *Pearl*, ca. 1922. 6.75" wall pocket, unmarked; 8.75" wall pocket, unmarked; 7.75" wall pocket, die-impressed WELLER. *Grant collection*. $250–350 (each)

Weller *Euclid*, ca. 1920s. Two 9.5" wall pockets, unmarked—one with cold-painted overglaze decoration (probably not done at the factory). *Grant collection*. $125–175 (each). This shape appears in a factory page that was reprinted in Huxford (page 366). The molded floral band is nearly identical to that used on the *Tivoli* wall pocket, but upside down.

Weller *Voile,* ca. 1911; *Klyro,* ca. 1925; and *Marvo,* ca. 1928. *Top: Voile* 6.25" x 7.25" wall pocket, black hand-painted 12X. *Middle: Klyro* 7" wall pocket, brown hand-painted W; *Marvo* 6.75" wall pocket, unmarked. *Bottom: Marvo* 7.5" wall pocket, round Weller Ware paper label. *Grant collection. Top:* $350–450. *Middle:* $150–200, 200–250. *Bottom:* $300–400

Weller *Lavonia,* ca. 1927; and Unknown Line, ca. 1920s. Two 10.75" wall pockets, unmarked. *Grant collection.* $350–400, $450–550

Weller *Klyro,* ca. 1925. 5.5" wall pocket, die-impressed WELLER; 8.25" wall pocket, blue hand-painted 2. *Grant collection.* $225–275, $300–400

Weller *Hobart,* ca. 1928; and *Lavonia,* ca. 1927. *Top: Lavonia* 8.5" wall pocket, unmarked. *Middle: Hobart* 12.5" wall pocket, die-impressed WELLER; *Lavonia* 12.5" wall pocket, inkstamp "half kiln" Weller Pottery mark. *Bottom: Hobart* 8.5" wall pocket, die-impressed WELLER. *Grant collection.* $300–400 (each, small), $550–650 (each, large)

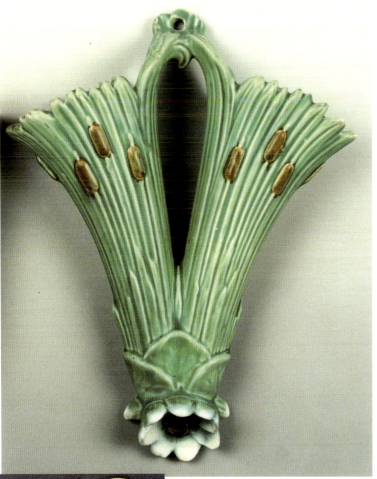

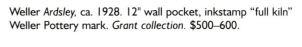

Weller *Ardsley,* ca. 1928. 12" wall pocket, inkstamp "full kiln" Weller Pottery mark. *Grant collection.* $500–600.

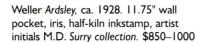

Weller *Ardsley,* ca. 1928. 11.75" wall pocket, iris, half-kiln inkstamp, artist initials M.D. *Surry collection.* $850–1000

Weller *Pumila,* ca. 1928. 7" wall pocket, unmarked. *Surry collection.* $400–500

Weller *Glendale,* ca. 1928. *Top:* 12.5" wall pocket, inkstamp "full kiln" Weller Pottery mark; 7" wall pocket, inkstamp scalloped WELLER WARE mark; 12.25" wall pocket, inkstamp "full kiln" Weller Pottery mark. *Bottom:* 7" wall pocket, inkstamp scalloped WELLER WARE mark. *Grant collection. Top:* $600–800, $500–600, $600–800. *Bottom:* $500–600. The shape at bottom can also be used as a free-standing vase.

Weller *Silvertone*, ca. 1928; and *Sabrinian*, ca. 1930. 10.5" wall pocket, inkstamp "half kiln" Weller Pottery mark; 8.25" wall pocket, inkstamp "half kiln" Weller Pottery mark. *Grant collection.* $600–700 (each)

Weller *Glendale*, ca. 1928. 7" wall pocket, with built-in flower frog, hand-painted 12X. *Hoppe collection.* $850–1000

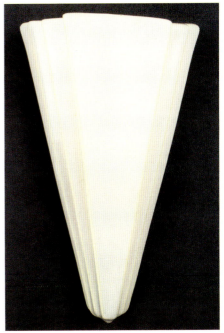

Weller *Lorbeek*, ca. 1928. 8.5" wall pocket, inkstamp "full kiln" Weller Ware mark. *Grant collection.* $375–475

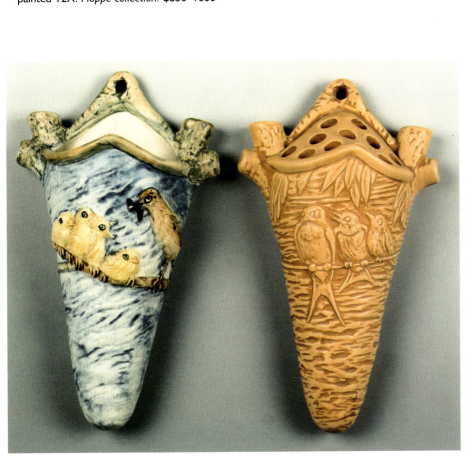

Weller *Glendale*, ca. 1928; and Unknown Maker. Weller *Glendale* 9" wall pocket, unmarked; 9" wall pocket, unmarked, derived in part from the Weller shape, maker unknown. *Grant collection.* $500–600, NPD (pending documentation of maker)

119

Weller Golden Glow, ca. 1932. 11.25" x 7" wall pocket, die-impressed Weller Pottery (script). Grant collection. $250–325

Weller Tutone, ca. 1930; Greora, ca. 1930; and Evergreen, ca. 1932. Tutone 10.5" wall pocket, black hand-painted 14; Greora 10.5" wall pocket, hand-incised Weller Pottery (script), black hand-painted 12; Evergreen 10.5" wall pocket, a Tutone shape, unmarked. Grant collection. $300–400, $400–500, $250–350

Weller Sydonia, ca. 1931. 9" wall pocket, double bud vase, black hand-painted 30; 9.75" wall pocket, quadruple bud vase, die-impressed Weller Pottery (script), black hand-painted 12. Grant collection. $275–350, $350–450

Weller Golden Glow, ca. 1932. 11.5" wall pocket, die-impressed Weller Pottery (script). Surry collection. $250–325. Note the additional coloring applied to the raised trim on this example.

Weller *Golden Glow*, ca. 1932. 8.5" planter on trellis, hand-incised X. *Surry collection*. $300–400

Weller *Novelty Line*, ca. 1934. Two 9.75" wall pockets, die-impressed Weller Pottery (script). *Grant collection*. $500–750 (each)

Weller *Malverne*, ca. 1930s. Two 11" wall pockets, die-impressed Weller Pottery (script). *Grant collection*. $300–400 (each)

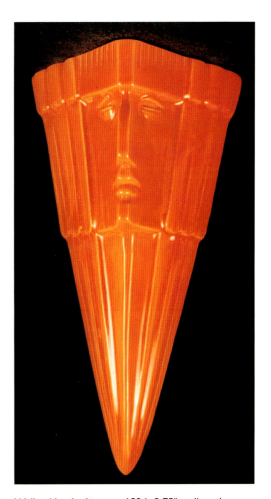

Weller *Novelty Line*, ca. 1934. 9.75" wall pocket, die-impressed Weller Pottery (script). *Mark Bassett Antiques, Lakewood, OH*. $500–750. This glossy orange color appears to be more scarce than the others used on this wall pocket.

121

Weller *Novelty Line*, ca. 1934. *Top:* 3" x 5.5" wall pocket; 8.5" x 9.25" wall pocket. *Middle:* Two 7.5" x 5.25" wall pockets. *Bottom:* 3" x 5.5" wall pocket; 8.5" x 9.25" wall pocket. *Grant collection. Top:* $200–250, $300–400. *Middle:* $275–350, $300–400. *Bottom:* $200–250, $300–400. All six examples are die-impressed Weller Pottery (script).

Weller *Bouquet*, ca. 1935; or *Blossom*, 1930s. *Top* and *Bottom:* Two 7" wall pockets, one with brown hand-painted 14 (bottom). *Middle:* 8.5" wall pocket, unmarked; 7" wall pocket, unmarked; 7" wall pocket, die-impressed WELLER; 8.5" wall pocket, unmarked. *Grant collection.* $125–175 (each, top and bottom), $150–200 (each, far left and far right), $175–250 (each, large)

Weller *Bouquet*, ca. 1935; or *Blossom*, 1930s. 7" wall pocket; 8.5" wall pocket—both unmarked. *Grant collection.* $125–175, $175–250. The difference between these two lines is not entirely clear.

Weller Unknown Lines, ca. 1930s. *Top:* Two 8" wall pockets, one with red hand-painted 14 (right). *Bottom:* Three 8" wall pockets, one with black hand-painted H (middle). *Grant collection.* $200–250 (each). Whether the bottom row forms part of the *Bouquet* line is not definitively known.

Weller *Classic,* ca. 1934. *Top:* Three 8" wall pockets. *Bottom:* Two 6.25" x 11" wall pockets. *Grant collection. Top:* $150–200, $125–175, $125–175. *Bottom:* $175–250 (each). All are die-impressed "Weller Pottery" (script) except the top left example, which is die-impressed "Weller Pottery Since 1872" (script). The top right example also has a paper *Classic* label.

Weller *Darsie,* ca. 1934. Two 8.75" wall pockets, die-impressed "Weller Pottery" (script). *Grant collection.* $150–200 (each)

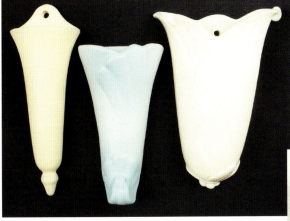

Weller *Arcadia,* ca. 1935; *Pastel,* ca. late 1930s; and Unknown Line, ca. 1920s. 9.5" wall pocket, unknown line, unmarked; *Pastel* 7.5" wall pocket, unmarked; *Arcadia* 8.75" wall pocket, die-impressed Weller Pottery / Since 1872 (script) and A-5. *Grant collection.* $125–175, $125–175, $150–200

Weller *Oak Leaf,* ca. 1930s. Three 8.5" wall pockets, die-impressed Weller Pottery (script), and with brown hand-painted letters DL (left), A (middle), and P (right). *Grant collection.* $150–225 (each)

Weller *Panella* and *Roba,* ca. late 1930s. *Top:* Two *Panella* 8" wall pockets, both die-impressed "Weller Pottery Since 1872" (script), one with brown hand-painted A (left). *Bottom:* Two *Roba* 10" wall pockets, both die-impressed "Weller Pottery Since 1872" (script), both with brown hand-painted letters, M (left) and R (right). *Grant collection.* Top: $175–225 (each). Bottom: $225–275 (each)

Western Stoneware, ca. 1920s or 1930s. 5.5" wall pocket, paper label reading MONMOUTH POTTERY. *Grant collection.* $75–100

Western Stoneware (or **Monmouth Pottery**, Monmouth, Illinois), ca. late 1920s. 12.25" wall pocket, Egyptian motifs, diamond-shaped black inkstamp reading WSC / MONMOUTH / ILL. *Surry collection.* $150–200

Western Stoneware, ca. 1930s. Three 9" wall pockets, unmarked. *Grant collection.* $125–150 (each). This shape appears in a 1930s catalog for Western Stoneware's "Monmouth Art Pottery" (in the collection of Robert and Lynn Herington).

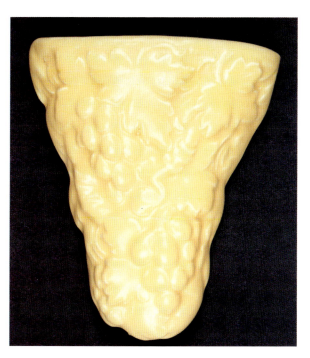

Western Stoneware, ca. 1941. 6.25" wall pocket, grapes, die-impressed logo in shape of shield with letters USA in triangular arrangement. *Surry collection.* $75–100. Shown in catalog page in Martin and Cooper (page 141).

Wheatley, ca. 1910–1920. 7.25" x 7" x 5" wall pocket, unmarked. *Grant collection.* $1200–1500. The leaves and grapes were hand-formed and applied onto a molded shape (shown in another photograph). Glaze skips like that at the top have little or no effect on value.

Wheatley Pottery (Cincinnati, Ohio), ca. 1910–1920. 8" x 9.25" x 5" wall pocket, unmarked. *Grant collection.* $1200–1500. Early examples of Wheatley are seldom marked; many reflect the influence of Grueby, as in this example. This example was probably molded, perhaps with hand-tooled details on the leaves.

Wheatley (attribution), ca. 1910–1920. 10" x 6.5" wall pocket, unmarked; 7" x 6.75" wall pocket, unmarked. *Grant collection.* $600–700 (each)

Wheatley, ca. 1920s or 1930s. 8.25" x 8" wall pocket, basket weave, die-impressed 11B / WP monogram. *Grant collection.* $700–800

Rick Wisecarver (Roseville, Ohio), 1981. Pair, 5.25" wall pockets, each hand-incised Wihoa's / Hand Made / Art Pottery / Rick Wisecarver / R.S. [Rick Sims] / 1981. *Grant collection.* $150–200 (each). Also well known as a painter on canvas, Rick Wisecarver passed away in 2002. Rick Sims was his life partner and often assisted him as a pottery decorator. The word "Wihoa" was coined by combining two family names: *Wisecarver* and *Hoadley*.

Wheatley, ca. 1920s or 1930s. 9.5" wall pocket, basket weave, die-impressed 278 / WP monogram. *Grant collection.* $700–800

Worthington (Crooksville, Ohio), ca. 1970s or later. Four 4.75" wall pockets, jug, unmarked. *Yonis collection.* $15–20 (each). This small concern is not mentioned in Lehner.

Wheatley, ca. 1920s or 1930s. 12.75" wall pocket, grapes, die-impressed 288 / WP monogram. *Surry collection.* $1200–1500

Chapter 3
Undocumented Wall Pockets

As Chapter 2 shows, the makers of many unmarked American art pottery wall pockets have been identified through scholarly research. Chapter 3 illustrates wall pockets whose maker is not yet known, although some shapes have been attributed to a particular maker by other writers.

To identify the maker of an unfamiliar and unmarked wall pocket, we begin with first-hand observation. Careful examination reveals clues about the methods of manufacture, the color of an item's clay body (after firing), its glaze characteristics, and its design style (for example, "Arts and Crafts" or "Art Deco"). These facts help us tentatively eliminate certain companies and narrow the field to a smaller group of possibilities.

As an example, consider the large matte green wall pocket with Art Nouveau thistles in low relief, shown here. The mottled glaze and Art Nouveau motif indicate a probable date of manufacture of ca. 1905-1915. (Comparable products by American firms can be dated to this period.) Buff-colored clay bodies are known to have been used with matte green glazes at several Zanesville, Ohio, potteries, and at Wheatley, of Cincinnati (see Chapter 2).

At this point, we are ready to turn to our shelf of reference books. Unfortunately, in the case of this particular wall pocket, investigation shows that this shape has not yet been documented by researchers. Without a credible factory document or other definitive evidence, we can do no more than offer an educated guess as to the wall pocket's maker—an attribution.

Researchers spend time in archives and microfilm to locate vintage images in the advertisements and trade catalogs of American potteries. They also study hundreds if not thousands of examples first-hand. This diligence allows them to combine knowledge of vintage images with first-hand observation, and draw conclusions about methods of identifying manufacturers and their products. Because such conclusions are based at least in part on theoretical assumptions (particularly when factory catalogs are unavailable), mistaken attributions can creep into even the most carefully assembled books. Space considerations allow researchers to reproduce only selected examples of vintage documents in their publications.

To be accurate, make your attributions explicit and unambiguous. Scholars and museum curators recommend using the word *attribution* in such cases. As a kind of shorthand, sellers describing an auction lot or preparing a price tag sometimes signal an attribution by enclosing a question mark in parentheses after the name of the maker to whom they have attributed the item in question.

It is difficult to estimate the value of an object whose maker is not known. Overall size and decorative value can be judged independently of maker, as can condition. The decorative style can offer hints to the probable dates of manufacture. These traits are weighed against the value of comparable items in order to estimate value. Until the makers of the items illustrated in Chapter 3 have been identified, the values shown here should be considered tentative.

The careful reader will also discover that Chapters 2 and 3 of *American Art Pottery Wall Pockets* make corrections to attributions made in older reference books—including

Maker Unknown, ca. 1905–1915. 14" x 7.75" wall pocket, Art Nouveau thistles, lime deposits on glaze, unmarked. *Grant collection.* $1200–1500 (tentative value). Buff-colored clay can be seen on the back of this example; the glaze is reminiscent of Roseville. However, Wheatley and Weller also used a buff-colored clay body.

the books on wall pockets. Whenever documentation was lacking or questionable, the terms *attribution* or *maker unknown* have been used in this book.

Maker Unknown, ca. 1910–1930. 10.25" wall pocket, roses, unmarked. *Grant collection.* $100–150 (tentative value). The glossy pink background is reminiscent of the 1920s, an era when both Weller and Roseville offered lines decorated with roses.

Maker Unknown, ca. 1910–1930. 8.5" wall pocket, cone shape, die-impressed 49. *Grant collection.* $100–150 (tentative value). This design may have been made by Zanesville Stoneware Company; the shape also resembles products made by Cliftwood, and one attributed to J.B. Owens.

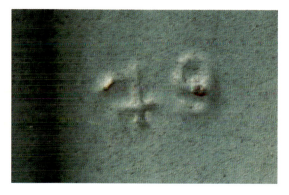

Mark from Matt Green Cone-Shaped Wall Pocket.

128

Maker Unknown, ca. 1910–1930. 9.75" wall pocket, vine-like motif with textured background details, unmarked. *Surry collection.* $100–150 (tentative value). The paneled body is reminiscent of the 1920s. Similar blended airbrushed coloring was used by various companies into the 1930s.

Maker Unknown, ca. 1915–1930. 8.5" wall pocket, grape vine, unmarked. *Courtesy of Cincinnati Art Galleries.* $100–150 (tentative value). This wall pocket is sometimes misidentified as Roseville *Sylvan*. It is not a Roseville product. (There is no wall pocket in Roseville's *Sylvan* line.) Some collectors attribute it to Weller, although no Weller line is known to use this style of decoration.

Maker Unknown, ca. 1910–present. 7.5" wall pocket; 8" wall pocket; 7.75" wall pocket; 5" wall pocket—all unmarked. *Grant collection.* $150–200, $150–200, $150–200, $200–300 (or $400–500, if made by Niloak). The far right example has been attributed to Niloak, but over 20 additional makers of "swirl" ware are known. For illustrated examples of Badlands, Evans/Desert Sands, Denver's White, Ozark, Silver Springs (Graack), and Muscle Shoals, see Gifford, *The Collector's Encyclopedia of Niloak* (pages 118–121).

Maker Unknown, ca. 1915–1930. 8.75" x 4.75" wall pocket, unmarked. *Grant collection.* $250–300 (tentative value). This shape is attributed to Weller by the Huxfords, who call it an example of the early *Golbogreen* line. (The wall pocket's maker surely also made the "U.S. MAIL" letter holder, shown on page 130.) In the January–February 2000 issue of the *Journal of the American Art Pottery Association* (page 10), Allan Wunsch illustrates a Scio (Ohio) China Co. paper label found on a candlestick the Huxfords had also dubbed "Golbogreen" (for the shape, see Huxford, page 315, row 4, item 1). With the Scio label as evidence, most collectors now feel that several pieces in the Huxfords' section on "Golbogreen" were actually made by Scio, not Weller. Because this wall pocket and letter holder (plus several other items shown in Huxford) have a different coloring and a more textural surface, a third manufacturer may have made them instead.

Maker Unknown, ca. 1915–1930. 7.25" x 6" letter holder, unmarked. *Grant collection.* $300–400 (tentative value). This shape is also known in a glossy green majolica-type glaze. Although the shape is attributed to Weller by the Huxfords (page 215), documentation is needed.

Maker Unknown, ca. 1920–1940. Four 8.5" wall pockets, unmarked. *Grant collection.* $125–175 (each, tentative value). The glaze on the top left example is similar to that found on Hull *Early Art* pieces. Martha and Steve Sanford attribute the shape to Peters and Reed (page 64), because the shape's outline resembles several known Peters and Reed wall pockets. Many American potteries produced lustre glazes during the 1920s. More research is needed.

Maker Unknown, ca. 1920–1940. 7.75" wall pocket, unmarked. *Mark Bassett Antiques, Lakewood, OH.* $75–100 (tentative value). Several companies produced a pale grayish blue glaze during the 1930s. Simple Arts and Crafts shapes like this were still being made in the 1920s and after by such companies as Cliftwood, Haeger, and Alamo.

Maker Unknown, ca. 1920s or later. 8" wall pocket, light gray clay, unmarked. *Grant collection.* NPD. This piece can also be used as a free-standing vase. The glaze is reminiscent of Fulper, although the shape has not been documented, and Fulper is usually marked. If made recently, the value would be $50 or less. If made by Fulper, the value would be at least $150.

Maker Unknown, ca. 1920–1940. 7" wall pocket, unmarked. *Surry collection.* $60–75 (tentative value). The unevenly applied glaze on this example indicates that it was made by a company on the order of Shawnee or McCoy, although no documentation is known to indicate the maker.

Maker Unknown, ca. 1930–1950. 16.5" wall pocket, double lily, die-impressed 651 / USA. *Surry collection.* $150–200 (tentative value). In Gibson (Book II), another example of this shape (perhaps a different size) is shown with hand-painted marks reading 0193 / ITALY / PV. The American example could be a Haeger or Camark product. It is remarkable that such a detailed shape remains without damage today.

Maker Unknown, ca. 1920–1940. 9" x 5.75" wall pocket, brick red clay, unmarked. *Grant collection.* $100–150 (tentative value). This example has a classical Roman motif, and could have been made in almost any season. The blended glossy brown and green glaze seems typical of the period indicated.

Maker Unknown, ca. 1950–1960. Two 10.5" birdhouse wall pockets, white and chartreuse, both die-impressed 711, both buff clay. *Grant collection.* NPD. Shape 711 appears in Abingdon's 1950 catalog, the last year that company made artware. The Abingdon birdhouse wall pocket should be valued at $85–100. However, the two examples illustrated here have buff clay instead of the white clay characteristic of Abingdon. Some examples of the shape bear a ribbon-shaped foil Roseville label that is otherwise known only on a few *Mock Orange* shapes. Further research is needed.

Maker Unknown, ca. 1950–1970. *Top Center:* 5" wall pocket, boot, die-impressed USA. *Middle* and *Bottom:* Three 4" wall pockets, pair of boots, die-impressed USA. *Surry collection. Top Center:* $12–15. *Other:* $15–20 (each). These wall pockets have dark buff clay, as do the butterfly and fish wall pockets also shown here. All are believed to be products of the same maker, possibly Dryden.

Maker Unknown, ca. 1950–1970. 4.25" x 5.25" wall pocket, butterfly, unmarked. *Surry collection.* $25–35

Maker Unknown, ca. 1950–1970. 5.5" wall pocket, fish, unmarked. *Surry collection.* $20–30. During the 1950s many American potteries developed lines of products that seemed likely to appeal more to men, than to women (such were the gender stereotypes of yesteryear).

Chapter 4
Other Hanging Items

Other hanging pieces—such as letter, match, and toothbrush holders, masks, plaques, sconces, and shelves—make interesting additions to a wall pocket collection. In this chapter, an assortment of such items is illustrated.

Note: Some authors and collectors define the term "wall pockets" broadly enough to apply to many of these shape families too.

Cambridge (attribution), ca. 1907–1910. 7.5" x 5" wall sconce, triangular, applied leaf, unmarked. *Grant collection.* $300–400

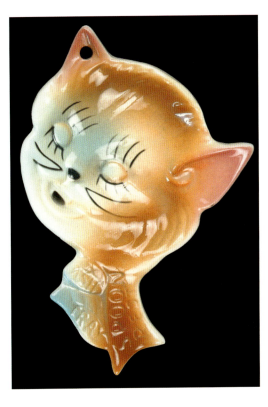

Cookson Pottery (Roseville, Ohio), ca. 1950s or 1960s. 7.5" ashtray or spoon rest, cat, unmarked. *Yonis collection.* $15–20. Designed by Louise Bauer, and purchased at her estate auction in Zanesville, July 2001.

Cochiti Pueblo, ca. 1950s–1980s. 6.75" x 5" match holder, unmarked, ca. 1980s; 6" x 4" match holder, pencil "Ada Buena / Cochita," ca. 1950s. *Grant collection.* $850–1000, $1000–1250. The makers, age, and current market value of Native American ceramics are difficult to determine, but Barry provides useful background information.

Frankoma, ca. 1942–1989. *Top:* 5.5" mask 134, Oriental man; 3.75" small mask 135, Indian; 4.75" mask 133, Oriental woman. *Middle:* 5.25" mask 131, Indian; 4.25" mask G132, Indian maiden. *Bottom:* 6.75" mask 125, African man; 3.25" small mask, African man; 6.5" mask 124, African woman. *Private collection. Top:* $400–500, $75–100, $400–500. *Middle:* $100–125 (each). *Bottom:* $125–175, $250–300, $125–175

Frankoma, ca. 1942–1988. 6.5" vase 59, canteen, with leather thong to allow hanging. *Private collection.* $15–25. Examples of this shape with buff-colored clay are valued at about $25–50.

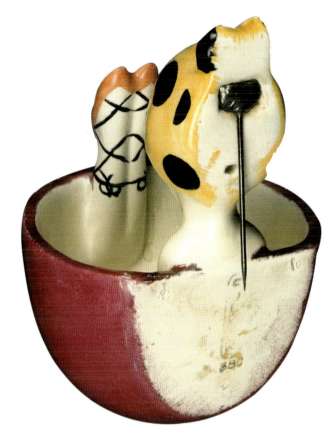

Another View of Fulper Upholstery Ashtray. The pin (often missing) allows this piece to hang on the arm of an upholstered armchair.

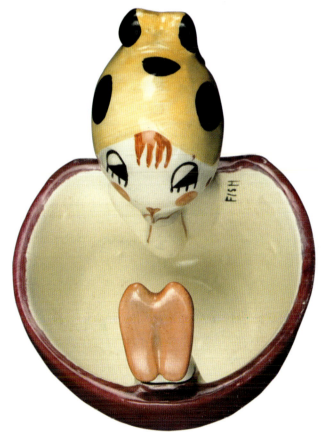

Fulper, ca. 1925. 4.75" upholstery ashtray, shape 380, designed by Ann H. Fish, vertical "racetrack" FULPER inkstamp / 380, artist signature FISH. *Courtesy of Mike Nickel and Cindy Horvath.* $700–800

Grueby Faience, ca. 1897–1907. Two 5.25" x 6" masks, rams, unmarked. *Grant collection.* $2200–2500 (each). These pieces were attributed to Grueby by David Rago, of *www.ragoarts.com*.

Hull *Bow-Knot,* ca. 1949. 10" wall plaque, die-impressed Hull Art / B-28-10 and hand-incised 15. *Yonis collection.* $850–1000

Hopi, ca. 1920s–1960s. 6.25" x 5.75" hanging basket, unmarked, ca. 1920s; 5" hanging match holder, unmarked, ca. 1950s or 1960s. *Grant collection.* $800–1000, $400–500

Hull *Bow-Knot,* ca. 1949. 10" wall plaque, die-impressed Hull Art / B-28-10. *Yonis collection.* $850–1000

Hull *Butterfly,* ca. 1956. 16" lavabo with metal rack, top die-impressed Hull (script) / USA and B24; bottom die-impressed Hull (script) / USA and B25 / © '56. *Yonis collection.* $175–225. For a photograph that illustrates the original rack more clearly, see Roberts, page 117.

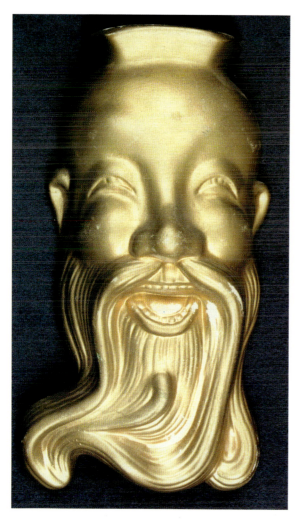

Hull *Gold Medal*, ca. 1960s. 8" wall mask, Chinese Sage, die-impressed Hull (script) / USA and 120. *Yonis collection.* $100–150

McCoy (Mt. Clemens era), ca. 1970s. Four 5.5" hanging match holders, top left example die-impressed 151 / USA on base; others die-impressed 151 / McCoy / LCC / USA on back. *Lindberg collection.* $30–40 (each). This shape can also be used as a vase or wall pocket.

McCoy, ca. 1940s. 7" x 9.25" tile, original frame, unmarked. *Courtesy of Jeff Koehler.* $9500–11,000. This rare Nelson McCoy shape saw only a limited production. In July 2002, this example was sold at auction by Jeff Koehler Real Estate and Auction Company (Zanesville, Ohio) for $9900 (including a 10% buyer premium).

McCoy (Mt. Clemens era), ca. 1979. 8" wall pocket, grater, unmarked. *Lindberg collection.* $40–50. This shape was intended to hold wooden kitchen utensils.

McCoy (Mt. Clemens era), ca. 1970s–1980s. Two 11.75" wall sconces 153, brown example die-impressed 153 USA; white example unmarked. *Lindberg collection.* $30–40 (each). The sconce was merely glued in place, so is sometimes missing (as shown in the brown example).

Rookwood, designed ca. 1909. Two 11.5" x 6.25" wall sconces 1688, designed by Sarah ("Sallie") Toohey, undated, triangle esoteric mark; and undated, die-impressed X2498X. *Grant collection.* $2000–2500 (each)

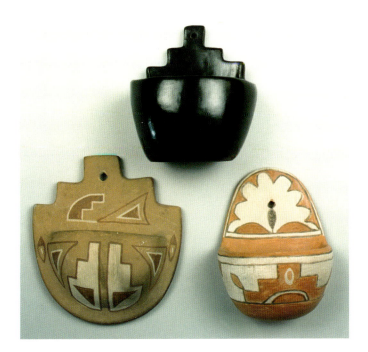

Native American (various makers), ca. 1940s–1970s. *Top:* Santa Clara 4" hanging basket, pencil signature Martha Mirabal / Santa Clara, age unknown. *Bottom:* Jemez Pueblo (attribution) 5" hanging basket, unmarked, ca. 1940s or 1950s; San Juan Pueblo (attribution) 4.25" hanging basket, unmarked, ca. 1970s. *Grant collection. Top:* $600–750. *Bottom:* $450–550, $400–500

Rookwood, designed ca. 1910. 4.5" x 4.25" match holder 1754, heraldic lions rampant, designed by Sarah ("Sallie") Toohey, die-impressed S.T. in rectangle, dated X (1910); and 8.75" x 4.25" wall sconce 1760, roses, designed by Sarah ("Sallie") Toohey, dated XIX (1919). *Grant collection.* $1000–1200, $1200–1500

Rookwood (attribution), designed ca. 1915. 2.5" x 3" match holder, child's face, attributed to Rookwood by Riley Humler of www.cincinnatiartgalleries.com, die-impressed only ELLA KELLEY and dated 3-26-15. *Grant collection.* $1000–1200. Some unrecorded Rookwood shapes were commissioned for special occasions or to advertise a commercial concern. This example appears to commemorate a child's birth or christening.

Rookwood, designed ca. 1947. 8.5" holy water font 6975, St. Francis, designed by Clotilda Zanetta, dated XLVII (1947). *Courtesy of Cincinnati Art Galleries.* $150–200

Roseville *Creamware (Decorated)*, ca. 1905–1910. 16.75" x 6.75" wall sconce, shape E61, no factory mark. *Grant collection.* $5000–5500

Rookwood, designed ca. 1916. 8.75" x 6.75" wall fountain 2339, designed by Ernest Bruce Haswell, dated XVI (1916), die-impressed P for Soft Porcelain body. *Grant collection.* $1500–1800

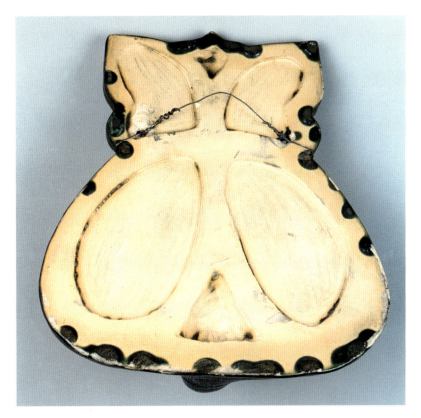

Roseville *Matt Green*, ca. 1905–1910. 16.75" wall sconce, shape E61, no factory mark. *Johnson collection.* $3500–4000

Another View of the E62 Wall Sconce.

Roseville *Matt Green*, ca. 1905–1910. 11" x 9.5" wall sconce, shape E62, no factory mark. *Johnson collection.* $2500–3000

Roseville *Matt Green*, ca. 1905–1910. 11" x 9.5" wall sconce, shape E62, no factory mark. *Hoppe collection.* $2500–3000

Roseville *Cameo*, ca. 1908. 12" wall sconce, shape 339, black TRPCo inkstamp. *Johnson collection.* $3000-3500 (with hairline; or $4750-5250 mint)

Roseville *Matt Green*, ca. 1908–1910. 9.25" x 8.25" wall mask, Ariadne, shape 345, no factory mark. *Grant collection.* $4000–5000

Roseville *Matt Green*, ca. 1908–1910. 12" corner wall sconce, shape 344, no factory mark. *Hoppe collection.* $2750–3250

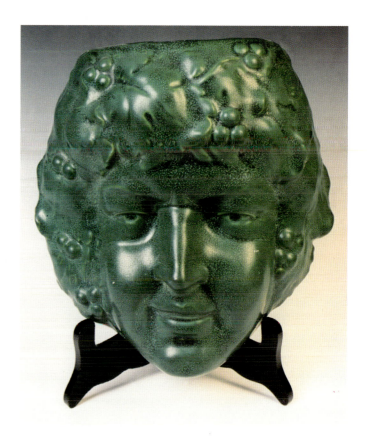

Roseville *Matt Green*, ca. 1908–1910. 9.5" wall mask, Bacchus, shape 346, no factory mark. *Hoppe collection.* $4000–5000

Roseville *Pine Cone*, ca. 1936. Three 288-7" wall plaques, no factory mark. *Johnson collection.* $700–800 (green), $900–1100 (brown or blue)

Roseville *Iris*, ca. 1939. Three wall shelves, shape 2. *Johnson collection.* $600–700 (each). Die-impressed "Roseville" and 2.

Roseville *Pine Cone*, ca. 1938–1939. Three 5" x 8" wall shelves, shape 1. *Johnson collection.* $850–1000 (blue), $650–750 (green or brown). Die-impressed "Roseville" and "No 1."

Roseville *Ivory* and *Crystal Green*, ca. 1939. Two 4.5" x 5.5" wall shelves, shape 3. *Johnson collection.* $250–300 (Ivory), $350–450 (Crystal Green). Die-impressed "Roseville" and 3.

Roseville *Burmese*, ca. 1950. *Top:* Three 72B wall masks. *Bottom:* three 82B wall masks. *Johnson collection.* $275–350 (each). Raised-relief (molded) factory marks.

Van Briggle, ca. 1920s. 4.5" match holder, Persian Rose, hand-incised AA monogram / VAN BRIGGLE / Colo. Spgs. *Grant collection.* $275–350

Sandia Pueblo, ca. 1990s. 10.25" x 6.75" match holder, hand-incised "Vicky T. Calabaza"; 7.5" x 5.25" match holder, hand-painted "J.D. IT. Lujan / Sandia Pue., NM." *Grant collection.* $450–600 (each)

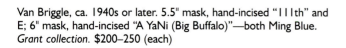

Van Briggle, ca. 1940s or later. 5.5" mask, hand-incised "111th" and E; 6" mask, hand-incised "A YaNi (Big Buffalo)"—both Ming Blue. *Grant collection.* $200–250 (each)

Weller *Etna,* ca. 1905. 2.5" x 3" miniature advertising wall plaque, lettering reads WELLER POTTERY 1905, unmarked. *Grant collection.* $1200–1500

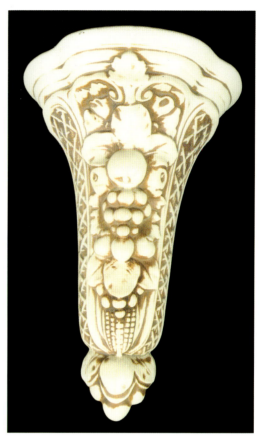

Weller *Ivory,* ca. 1910. 9.5" x 6.75" x 4.25" wall shelf, die-impressed WELLER (small capitals). *Courtesy of McAllister Auctions.* $400–500

Weller *Ivory,* ca. 1910. 12.25" wall shelf, die-impressed RL (initials of designer, Rudolf Lorber). *Grant collection.* $500-600

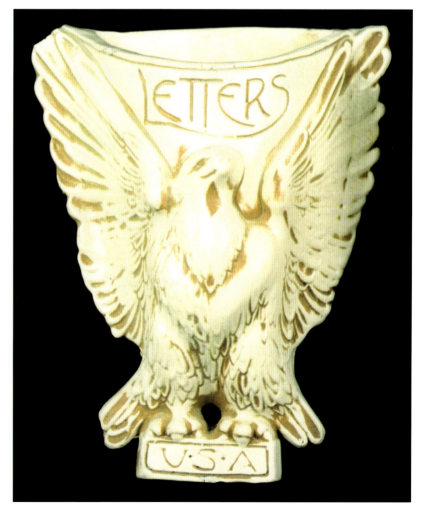

Weller *Ivory,* ca. 1910. 8.75" x 7.25" letter holder, die-impressed WELLER (stylized lettering), paper White Pillars Museum label. *Grant collection.* $600–800

Weller *Flemish*, ca. 1917. 7.25" toothbrush holder; 7.5" brush holder; 7.5" match holder with strike pad—all die-impressed WELLER. *Grant collection.* $1000–1250 (each). Two of these items (left and middle) also have paper White Pillars Museum labels.

Weller *Creamware*, ca. 1910. 7" toothbrush holder, die-impressed WELLER. *Grant collection.* $550–650. Weller's hanging toiletry items are rare.

Worthingon. 9.5" x 5.25" oval platter (or wall plaque), "Turkey in the Straw," artist monogram BY BEE. *Yonis collection.* $60–75

Weller *Roma*, ca. 1912; and *Creamware*. Roma 4.5" x 7.5" x 3.25" letter holder, unmarked; *Creamware* 7.5" match holder, die-impressed WELLER. *Grant collection.* $600–700, $450–550

Weller *Novelty Line,* ca. 1934. Three 10" x 7" flowerpot holders, two missing their flowerpot. *Grant collection.* $250–350 (without flowerpot), $300–400 (complete set). The middle example is die-impressed Weller Pottery (script) on both the pot and the holder.

Weller *Woodcraft,* ca. 1930s. 13.5" garden ornament, running squirrel, unmarked. *Grant collection.* $1400–1600. An October 1930 factory advertisement in *Gift and Art Buyer* (page 44) describes this figure as "life-size. Can scarcely be detected from the real when at a distance on a [tree] limb."

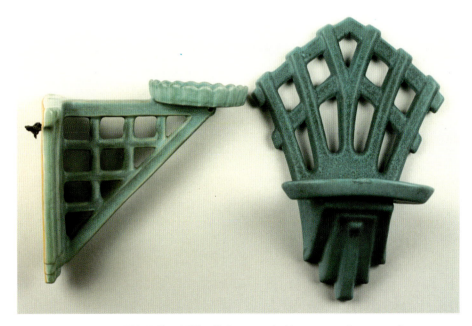

Weller *Evergreen,* ca. 1932. 7.5" x 5.75" x 0" flowerpot holder, missing the pot; and 11.25" x 8" x 5" flowerpot holder, missing the pot—both die-impressed Weller Pottery (script). *Grant collection.* $300–400 each (or $400–500 each, with the original flowerpot).

Another View of *Woodcraft* Squirrel.

Chapter 5
Factory Marks

Some vintage American art pottery wall pockets have no factory mark. Marked examples can bear a permanently applied factory name or monogram; others can be marked with paper or foil labels. Some examples have a shape number, either die-impressed, hand-incised, inkstamp, or handwritten in pencil or crayon. Other marks whose meaning is not known today were also used by some companies.

This chapter illustrates a variety of factory marks, defining (by example) such terms as "die-impressed" and "hand-incised." *Caution:* Only a few known marks are illustrated here for any given company.

Although a familiarity with typical marks can help collectors identify makers, other complicating factors must be kept in mind. Many of the long-lived potteries—like McCoy, Roseville, and Weller—periodically changed both their trademarks and their methods of marking pieces. If a wall pocket was originally marked with a paper or foil label, years of use and cleaning may have caused the label to be lost. Some companies did not trouble themselves with marking their products. Recent reproductions often bear marks that resemble those used on authentic vintage examples.

Most collectors do not value marked examples more highly than unmarked pieces. They view intact paper labels and clear markings as an added bonus, although value is first determined according to such factors as rarity, glaze quality, condition, and so on.

Some recent reproduction Roseville wall pockets are marked in a manner that seems intended to deceive beginners. For color photographs of authentic and spurious marks that read "Roseville," plus all 132 vintage Roseville lines in each standard color variation, and representative reproductions, see my book *Introducing Roseville Pottery*.

For detailed information about marks used by American firms, consult one of the specialized reference books listed in the Selected Bibliography. *Note:* Before about 1995, authors of reference books usually published line drawings, instead of photographs, to illustrate factory marks.

Hand-Incised Marks from a Brown County Wall Pocket.

Hand-Painted Marks from a Brown County Hills Wall Pocket.

Die-Impressed Shape Number. This example is from a Brush wall pocket bearing no other identifying marks.

Die-Impressed Acorn Logo from an Oakwood Wall Pocket.

"Arkansas" Inkstamp and Paper Label from a Camark Wall Pocket.

Die-Impressed Marks from a Faenza Wall Pocket.

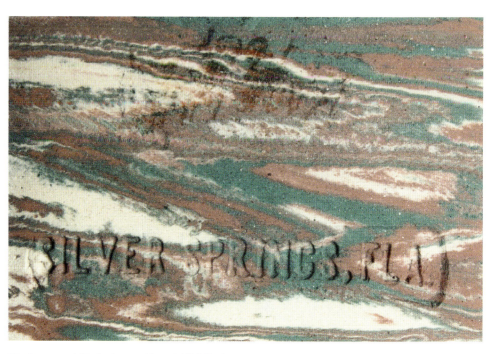
Die-Impressed Marks from a Graack Wall Pocket.

"Racetrack" Inkstamp from a Fulper Wall Pocket.

Die-Impressed Logo from a Grueby Wall Pocket.

Paper Label from a Fulper Fayence Wall Pocket.

Die-Impressed Marks from a Hampshire Wall Pocket.

Hand-Incised Mark from a Jervis Wall Pocket.

Hand-Incised Marks on an Indianapolis Terra Cotta Wall Pocket.

Die-Impressed Logo and Paper Label from a Marblehead Wall Pocket.

Hand-Incised Logo from an Overbeck Wall Pocket.

Hand-Incised Marks from a Muncie Wall Pocket.

Die-Impressed Marks from an Owens Wall Pocket.

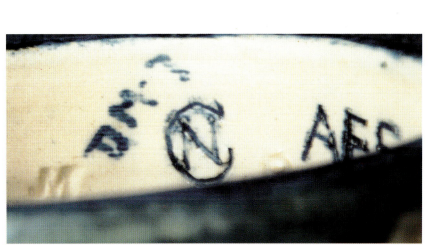
Hand-Painted and Die-Impressed Marks from a Newcomb Wall Pocket.

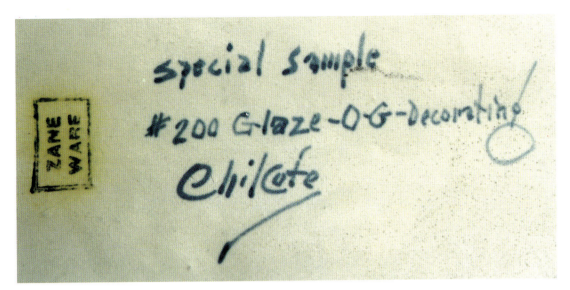

Hand-Painted and Inkstamp Marks from a Peters and Reed (or Zane) Wall Pocket.

Hand-Painted Marks from a Paul Revere/S.E.G. Wall Pocket.

Die-Impressed Logo and other Marks from a Rookwood Wall Pocket. Below the RP logo (surrounded by fourteen "flames," one for each year between 1886 and 1900), most wall pockets have a shape number, indicated by an Arabic numeral. These marks are followed by a date code in Roman numerals. The die-impressed "XV" in this example notes that the year of production was 1915. Between 1900 and the late 1950s, Rookwood marks generally include a die-impressed Roman numeral identifying the last two digits of the year of manufacture. Most Rookwood is also marked with a die-impressed Arabic numeral identifying the shape number. For more details, see Peck II.

Die-Impressed Logo from a Pewabic Wall Pocket. Note that the thick glazes used on some American art pottery required grinding at the factory to level a vase's foot (or a wall pocket's back). Such grinding is not considered damage, even if it causes some loss to the glaze at the edge of a piece.

151

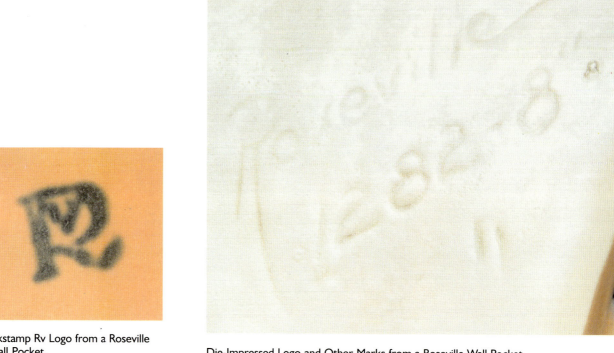

Inkstamp Rv Logo from a Roseville Wall Pocket.

Die-Impressed Logo and Other Marks from a Roseville Wall Pocket.

Foil Label from a Roseville Wall Pocket. *Caution:* In my research on Roseville, I have found several examples of pottery by a different company but bearing a vintage Roseville label on the base. Paper and foil labels can be removed by an unscrupulous seller and then glued onto another piece! When in doubt, examine the label for signs of disturbance, such as a crease or nicked edges.

Raised-Relief (Molded) Logo and Other Marks from a Roseville Wall Pocket.

Die-Impressed Logo and Other Marks from a Strobl Wall Pocket.

Hand-Incised Logo and Other Marks from a Van Briggle Wall Pocket.

Die-Impressed Marks from a Teco Wall Pocket.

153

Die-Impressed Mark from a Weller Wall Pocket.

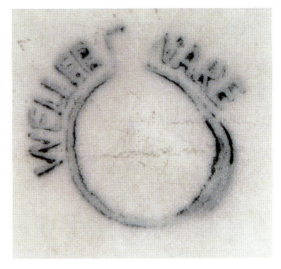

"Full Kiln" Inkstamp from a Weller Wall Pocket.

Scalloped Inkstamp from a Weller Wall Pocket.

"Half Kiln" Inkstamp and Foil Label from a Weller Wall Pocket.

Die-Impressed Marks from a Wheatley Wall Pocket.

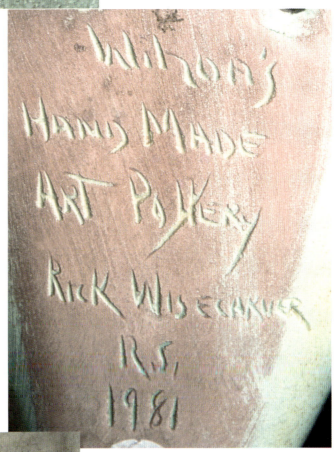

Hand-Incised Marks from a Wisecarver Wall Pocket.

Hand-Incised Mark (in script) from a Weller Wall Pocket.

Selected Bibliography

For readers interested in history, the following bibliography should prove useful, although it does *not* mention all titles published on any given subject. In general, this bibliography lists reference books that illustrate additional examples and/or reprint pertinent factory documents. An asterisk (*) identifies the reference books that illustrate at least one wall pocket or related items not shown in *American Art Pottery Wall Pockets*. Titles that are out of print can sometimes be borrowed through a metropolitan public library or university library; or purchased through used-book services on the Internet. Some books offer values; others do not.

Lehner's Encyclopedia is an essential reference book. If you have not already done so, I recommend purchasing a copy for your personal library. Most companies whose products are shown in *American Art Pottery Wall Pockets* also have an entry in *Lehner's*. For non-U.S. marks, consult Ralph and Terry Kovel, *Kovels' New Dictionary of Marks: Pottery and Porcelain, 1850 to the Present* (New York: Crown, 1986). One of the best general-purpose introductions to American art pottery and tile is *Kovels' American Art Pottery* (out of print). Paul Evans' *Art Pottery of the United States...* has a more limited scope, but is carefully researched and fully documented.

SPECIALIZED REFERENCE BOOKS

ABINGDON
*Paradis, Joe. *Abingdon Pottery Artware, 1934–1950: Stepchild of the Great Depression*. Atglen, Pennsylvania: Schiffer Publishing, 1997.

BRUSH-McCOY and BRUSH (originally J.W. McCOY)
*Sanford, Martha and Steve. *Sanfords Guide to Brush-McCoy Pottery, Book 1*. Campbell, California: Adelmore Press, 1992.
*___. *Sanfords Guide to Brush-McCoy Pottery, Book 2*. Campbell, California: Adelmore Press, 1996.

CAMARK
*Gifford, David Edwin. *Collector's Guide to Camark Pottery: Identification and Values*. Paducah, Kentucky: Collector Books, 1997.
*___. *Collector's Guide to Camark Pottery: Identification and Values: Book II*. Paducah, Kentucky: Collector Books, 1999.

CATALINA ISLAND POTTERY
*Coates, Carole. *Catalina Island Pottery and Tile, 1927-1937: Island Treasures*. Atglen, Pennsylvania: Schiffer Publishing, 2001.

CLIFTWOOD and MORTON
*Hall, Doris and Burdell. *Morton Potteries: 99 Years, Vol. 2*. Gas City, Indiana: L-W Book Sales, 1995.

COWAN
*Bassett, Mark and Victoria Naumann. *Cowan Pottery and the Cleveland School*. Atglen, Pennsylvania: Schiffer Publishing, 1997.

FRANKOMA
*Schaum, Gary V. *Collector's Guide to Frankoma Pottery, 1933 through 1990: Identifying Your Collection, Including Gracetone*. 1997; 3rd. Printing. Gas City, Indiana: L-W Book Sales, 2001.

KAY FINCH
*Nickel, Mike and Cindy Horvath. *Kay Finch Ceramics: Her Enchanted World*. Atglen, Pennsylvania: Schiffer Publishing, 1996.

FULPER and STANGL
Hibel, John, Carole Goldman Hibel, and Robert De Falco. *The Fulper Book*. State College, Pennsylvania: Nittany Valley Offset Press, [1986].
*Runge, Robert C., Jr. *Collector's Encyclopedia of Stangl Artware, Lamps, and Birds: Identification and Values*. Paducah, Kentucky: Collector Books, 2002.

GRUEBY
Montgomery, Susan J. *The Ceramics of William H. Grueby: The Spirit of the New Idea in Artistic Handicraft*. Lambertville, New Jersey: Arts and Crafts Quarterly Press, 1993.

HAEGER and ROYAL HAEGER
*Dilley, David D. *Haeger Potteries: Through the Years: A Price Guide*. Gas City, Indiana: L-W Book Sales, 1997.
*Paradis, Joe and Joyce. *The House of Haeger, 1914-1944: The Revitalization of American Art Pottery*. Atglen, Pennsylvania: Schiffer Publishing, 1999.

HULL
Roberts, Brenda. *Collector's Encyclopedia of Hull Pottery*. Paducah, Kentucky: Collector Books, 1980.

LENOX
*Morin, Richard E. *Lenox Collectibles*. Tulsa, Oklahoma: Sixty-Ninth Street Zoo, 1993.

Robinson, Dorothy [Nolan], with Bill Feeny. *The Official Price Guide to American Pottery and Porcelain*. Ed. Thomas E. Hudgeons III. Orlando, Florida: House of Collectibles, [1980]. [Illustrated guide to the ceramics made in Trenton, New Jersey, particularly Lenox.]

NELSON McCOY
*Sanford, Martha and Steve. *Sanfords Guide to McCoy Pottery*. Campbell, California: Adelmore Press, 1997.

*Snyder, Jeffrey B. *McCoy Pottery: A Field Guide*. Atglen, Pennsylvania: Schiffer Publishing, 2002.

NATIVE AMERICAN
Barry, John W. *American Indian Pottery: An Identification and Value Guide*. Florence, Alabama: Books Americana, 1981.

NICODEMUS
*Riebel, Jim. *Sanfords Guide to Nicodemus: His Pottery and His Art*. Campbell, California: Adelmore Press, 1998.

MUNCIE
*Rans, Jon and Mark Eckelman. *Collector's Encyclopedia of Muncie Pottery: Identification and Values*. Paducah, Kentucky: Collector Books, 1999.

NEWCOMB
Poesch, Jessie. *Newcomb Pottery: An Enterprise for Southern Women, 1895-1940*. Atglen, Pennsylvania: Schiffer Publishing, 1984.

NILOAK
*Gifford, David Edwin. *Collector's Encyclopedia of Niloak: A Reference and Value Guide*. 1993; rev. 2nd ed. Paducah, Kentucky: Collector Books, 2001.

J. B. OWENS
Hahn, Frank L. *Collector's Guide to Owens Pottery* ... Lima, Ohio: Golden Era Publications, 1996.

PETERS AND REED and ZANE
*Sanford, Martha and Steve. *Sanfords Guide to Peters and Reed and Zane Pottery*. Campbell, California: Adelmore Press, 2000.

PEWABIC
Pears, Lillian Myers. *The Pewabic Pottery: A History of Its Products and Its People*. Des Moine, Iowa: Wallace-Homestead Book Co., 1976.

RED WING and RUMRILL
*Reiss, Ray. *Red Wing Art Pottery: Classic American Pottery from the 30s, 40s, 50s and 60s: Including Pottery Made for RumRill*. Chicago: Property [Ray Reiss], 1996.

*___. *Red Wing Art Pottery Two: Including Pottery Made for RumRill*. Chicago: Property [Ray Reiss], 2000.

ROBINSON RANSBOTTOM
*Skillman, Sharon and Larry. *Sanfords Guide to the Robinson Ransbottom Pottery Co.* Campbell, California: Adelmore Press, [2001].

ROOKWOOD
*Peck, Herbert. *The Second Book of Rookwood Pottery*. Tucson, Arizona: Herbert Peck, 1968. [No values. Numerical shape guide. Many additional wall pocket shapes are shown as line drawings. No photographs.]

ROSEMEADE
*Dommel, Darlene Hurst. *Collector's Encyclopedia of Rosemeade Pottery: Identification and Values*. Paducah, Kentucky: Collector Books, 2000.

ROSEVILLE
Bassett, Mark. *Bassett's Roseville Prices*. 2nd ed. Atglen, Pennsylvania: Schiffer Publishing, 2001. [No illustrations. Values for Roseville products, including wall pockets, arranged alphabetically by line name.]

*___. *Introducing Roseville Pottery*. 1999; Rev. 2nd ed. Atglen, Pennsylvania: Schiffer Publishing, 2001. [Alphabetical guide to the standard Roseville patterns and colors. Includes accurate chronology and photographs of Roseville marks. A rare early Roseville *Apple Blossom* and a fake *Luffa* wall pocket are shown.]

___. *Understanding Roseville Pottery*. Atglen, Pennsylvania: Schiffer Publishing, 2002. [A fake *Panel* wall pocket with a nude figure is shown, along with the fake mark.]

*Bomm, Jack and Nancy. *Roseville in All Its Splendor*. 1998; 2nd ed. Gas City, Indiana: L-W Book Sales, 2000. [Reprints 100's of factory pages, many of which include a wall pocket.]

Huxford, Sharon and Bob, and Mike Nickel. *Collector's Encyclopedia of Roseville Pottery*. Vol. 2. 1976; Rev. ed. Paducah, Kentucky: Collector Books, 2001. [No additional wall pockets are shown, although a Roseville *Cameo* letter holder appears on page 179.]

ROYAL COPLEY and SPAULDING
*Schneider, Mike. *Royal Copley: Identification and Price Guide*. Atglen, Pennsylvania: Schiffer Publishing, 1995.

SHAWNEE
*Curran, Pamela Duvall. *Shawnee Pottery: The Full Encyclopedia*. Atglen, Pennsylvania: Schiffer Publishing, 1995.

TECO

*Darling, Sharon S. *Teco: Art Pottery of the Prairie School*. Erie, Pennsylvania: Erie Art Museum, 1989.

VAN BRIGGLE

Sasicki, Richard, and Josie Fania. *Collector's Encyclopedia of Van Briggle Art Pottery: An Identification and Value Guide*. Paducah, Kentucky: Collector Books, 1993.

WALL POCKETS

*Gibson, Joy and Marvin. *Collectors Guide to Wall Pockets: Affordable, Unique and Other$, Book II*. Gas City, Indiana: L-W Book Sales, 1997.

[Survey of ceramic, glass, metal, plastic, and other wall pockets from the U.S. and other countries. Includes corrections to the Gibsons' earlier book. Many additional American wall pockets are shown, by such makers as Abingdon; American Art Pottery (Morton, Illinois); American Pottery (Marietta, Ohio); Johannes Brahm (Los Angeles); Brush McCoy/Brush; California Art Products (Los Angeles); California Cleminsons (El Monte); Camark; Cliftwood; A.R. Cole (Sanford, North Carolina); Coventry Ware (Barberton, Ohio); deLee Art (Hollywood, California); Dryden; Freeman-McFarlin Potteries (El Monte, California); Gilner (Culver City, California); Goldra (East Palestine, Ohio); Haeger; Heirlooms of Tomorrow/California Originals (Manhattan Beach and Torrance, California); Hollywood Ceramics (Los Angeles); Hull; Klay Kraft (Milford, Nebraska); Loveland Art Pottery (Loveland, Colorado); Marsh Industries (Los Angeles); Metlox (Manhattan Beach, California); Miramar of California (Los Angeles); Ohio Porcelain (Zanesville); Pfaltzgraff; Red Wing; Rocky Mountain; Royal Copley/Spaulding China; Shawnee; Stanford; Stangl; Walter Starnes (Los Angeles); Treasure Craft (South Gate, California); Walker Potteries (Monrovia, California); Weil of California (Los Angeles); and others.]

*Gibson, Marvin and Joy. *Collectors Guide to Wall Pockets: Affordable and Other$*. Gas City, Indiana: L-W Book Sales, 1994.

[Survey of ceramic, glass, metal, plastic, and other wall pockets from the U.S. and other countries. Many additional American wall pockets are shown, by such makers as Block Pottery (Los Angeles); California Cleminsons; deLee Art; Ceramicraft (San Clemente, California); Coventry Ware; Gilner; Goldra; Haeger; Hollywood Ceramics; Hull; Kingwood Ceramics (East Palestine, Ohio); Knowles, Taylor & Knowles of California; Maurice Ceramics of California (Los Angeles); McCoy; Stewart B. McCulloch (California); Metlox; Morton; Red Wing; Rocky Mountain; Royal Copley/Spaulding China; Stanford; Treasure Craft; Weil of California; West Coast Pottery (Burbank, California); and others.]

*Newbound, Betty and Bill. *Collector's Encyclopedia of Wall Pockets: Identification and Values*. 1995; rpt. Paducah, Kentucky: Collector Books, 1998.

[Survey of ceramic, glass, metal, plastic, and other wall pockets from the U.S. and other countries. Many additional American wall pockets are shown, by such makers as Abingdon; California Cleminsons; Ceramicraft; Cherokee China (Jonesboro, Tennessee); deLee Art; Erwin Pottery (Erwin, Tennessee); Goldra; Haeger; Hull; McCoy; Stewart B. McCulloch; Maddux of California (Los Angeles); Metlox; Morton; Price and Keemer (Lancaster, Pennsylvania); Pennsbury (Morrisville, Pennsylvania); Royal Copley; Senegal China (Pelham, New York); Shawnee; Stanford; Treasure Craft; Williamsburg Pottery Factory (Lightfoot, Virginia); Walter Wilson (Pasadena, California); and others.]

*Perkins, Fredda. *Wall Pockets of the Past*. Paducah, Kentucky: Collector Books, 1996.

[Survey of ceramic, glass, metal, plastic, and other wall pockets from the U.S. and other countries. A few additional American wall pockets are shown, by such makers as Abingdon; Block; Brush; California Pottery Co.; Camark; Gilner; Hull; McCoy; Morton; Royal Copley; Shawnee; Treasure Craft; and others.]

WELLER

Carrigan, Linda, and Allan Wunsch. *Weller Pottery: The Rare, the Unusual, the Seldom Seen*. Sarasota, Florida: Marlin Media, 2003. [No values.]

*Huxford, Sharon and Bob. *The Collectors Encyclopedia of Weller Pottery*. Paducah, Kentucky: Collector Books, 1979.

McDonald, Ann Gilbert. *All About Weller: A History and Collector's Guide to Weller Pottery, Zanesville, Ohio*. Marietta, Ohio: Antique Publications, 1989.

GENERAL REFERENCE BOOKS

*Bess, Phyllis and Tom. *Frankoma and Other Oklahoma Potteries*. Atglen, Pennsylvania: Schiffer Publishing, 1995.
[Illustrated histories of Creek, Frankoma, Hammat Originals, Tamac, and other concerns.]

*Chipman, Jack. *Collectors' Encyclopedia of California Pottery*. 1992; Rev. and expanded 2nd edition. Paducah, Kentucky: Collector Books, 1999.
[Illustrated histories of Kay Finch, La Mirada, and other concerns, plus additional wall pockets or other hanging items by Sascha Brastoff, Catalina, Cleminsons, Florence, Gladding McBean, Hagen-Renaker, Haldeman, La Mirada, Padre, Weil of California, and Barbara Willis.]

Evans, Paul. *Art Pottery of the United States...* 1974; Rev. and Enlarged 2nd ed. New York: Feingold and Lewis, 1987.
[No values. Illustrated histories of George Ohr's Biloxi Art Pottery, California Faience, Cowan, Fulper, Grueby, Hampshire, Jervis, J.W. McCoy, Marblehead, Newcomb, Niloak, Overbeck, J.B. Owens, Paul Revere, Peters and Reed, Pewabic, Rookwood, Roseville, Strobl, Teco, Van Briggle, W.J. Walley, Weller, Wheatley Pottery, and other concerns.]

Henzke, Lucile. *Art Pottery of America*. 1982; 3rd ed. Atglen, Pennsylvania: Schiffer Publishing, 1999.
[Illustrated histories of Abingdon, Camark, Cambridge Art Pottery, Cordey, Cowan, Frankoma, Fulper/Stangl, Gates Pottery (that is, Teco), Grueby, Haeger, McCoy, Muncie, Newcomb, Niloak, J.B. Owens, Paul Revere, Peters and Reed/Zane, Pigeon Forge, Red Wing, Rookwood, Roseville, Van Briggle, Weller, Wheatley Pottery, and other concerns.]

Kovel, Ralph and Terry. *Kovels' American Art Pottery: The Collector's Guide to Makers, Marks, and Factory Histories*. New York: Crown Publishers, 1993.
[No values. Illustrated histories of Brush, California Faience, Camark, Cambridge Art Pottery, Cowan, Fulper, Grueby, Hampshire, Hull, Jervis, Marblehead, J.W. McCoy, Nelson McCoy, Newcomb, Niloak, George E. Ohr, Overbeck, Owens, Paul Revere, Peters and Reed, Pewabic, Red Wing, Rookwood, Roseville, Teco, Van Briggle, W.J. Walley, Weller, Wheatley Pottery, Zane, and other concerns.]

Lehner, Lois. *Lehner's Encyclopedia of U.S. Marks on Pottery, Porcelain and Clay*. Paducah, Kentucky: Collector Books, 1988.
[No values. Introductory-level discussions of 1000's of American makers. Only marks are illustrated, mostly as line drawings.]

*Royka, Paul. *Fireworks: New England Art Pottery of the Arts and Crafts Movement*. Atglen, Pennsylvania: Schiffer Publishing, 1997.
[Illustrated histories of Grueby, Hampshire, Marblehead, Merrimac, Paul Revere/Saturday Evening Girls, Walley, and a few additional New England potteries. One additional Walley wall pocket is shown.]

*Wiltshire, William E. III. *Folk Pottery of the Shenandoah Valley*. New York: E.P. Dutton, 1975.
[No values. Illustrated survey of late nineteenth century potters working in Maryland, Pennsylvania, Virginia, and West Virginia.]

Index of Makers

Boldface page numbers indicate illustrations.

Abingdon, 8, **9–10**, 131
Alamo, **10**, 130
American Ceramic Products, **10**
American Terra Cotta—see *Teco*
Associated American Artists—see *Stonelain*
Badlands, 129
Brown County, **11**, 146
Brown County Hills, **11**, 146
Bruen, 8
Brush (or Brush McCoy), 5, 8, **11–14**, 54, 55, **147**
Burley and Winter, **14**
California Art Products (or California Arts), **14**
California Faience, 8, **15**
Camark, 8, **15–17**, 131, **147**
Cambridge Art Pottery, 7, **17–18**, 54, **133**
Carillon China—see *General Ceramics*
Catalina Island, **18**
Chinese, **6**, 81, 86, 90, 91, 92, 93, 95
Clay Place, 8
Clay Trout, 8
Cliftwood, 8, **18–19**, 128, 130
Cochiti Pueblo—see *Native American*
Cookson, **133**
Cordey, **19**
Cowan, 8, **19–20**
Creek, **20**
Dadson, **20**
Desert Sands—see *Evans*
Diamond, **21**
Dryden, **21**, 132
Duffina, John E., **21**
Engelbreit, Mary, 8
English, 6
Ephraim Faience, 7, 8
Evans (or Desert Sands), 29
Faenza, **21**, **147**
Finch, Kay, **22**
Folk potters, 6
Frank X 2, **25**
Frankoma, 8, **22–25**, **133–134**
Frankoma Family Collectors Association, **25**
Fraunfelter, 15
Fulper, 4, 8, **26–28**, 30, 130, **134**, **148**
Gates—see *Teco*
General Ceramics, **29**
Graack, H.A., **29**, 129, **148**
Griffen, Smith and Hill, 6

Grueby, 7, 8, **29–30**, 125, **134**, **148**
Haeger (or Royal Haeger), 8, 28, **30–31**, **102**, 130, 131
Hammat, 31
Hampshire, 8, **31–32**, **149**
Hartnett, Michael, 8
Hines, 8
Hopi—see *Native American*
Hull, 4–5, 8, **32–36**, **135–136**
Hunter, Hannah, 8
Hyalyn, 8, **37**
Imai, Joy, 8
Indianapolis Terra Cotta, **37**, **149**
Italian, 131
James, J.D., 4–5
Japanese, 9
Jemez Pueblo—see *Native American*
Jervis, 7, **38**, **149**
Knowles, Taylor & Knowles (or KTK), **38**
La Mirada—see *American Ceramic Products*
Lenox, 8, **38–39**
Lessell—see *Camark* and *Weller*
McCoy (or Nelson McCoy), 4, 5, 8, **39–48**, 131, **136–137**, 146
Marblehead, 8, **49**, **149**
Monmouth—see *Western Stoneware*
Monterey, **50**
Morton (see also *Cliftwood*), **50–51**
Mountainside, **51**
Muncie, 8, **51**, **150**
Muscle Shoals, 129
Native American, **135**, **136**, **137**, **142**
Nelson McCoy—see *McCoy*
Newcomb College, 7, **52**, **150**
Nicodemus, **52**
Niloak, 8, **52**, 129
Oakwood, **17**, **147**
Ohr, George, 7, **53**
Overbeck, **55**, **150**
Owens, J.B., 7, 11, 15, **53–55**, 128, **150**
Ozark, 129
Paul Revere—see *S.E.G.*
Permian, **55**
Peters and Reed (or Zane), 8, **56–59**, 130, **151**
Pewabic, **59**, **151**
Pfaltzgraff, **59**
Pigeon Forge, **59**
Pine Hollow, 8
Red Wing, 8, **59–60**
Reproductions, 4–5, 40, 41, 43, 44, 81, 82, 86, 90, 91, 92, 93, 95, 146

Rice, Carolyn, 8
Robinson Ransbottom (or R.R.P. Co.), 8, **61**, 75
Rocky Mountain, **61**
Rookwood, 4, 5, 7, 8, 37, **62–67**, **137–138**, **151**
Rosemeade (or Wahpeton), **67–68**
Rosenberg, Toby, 8
Roseville, 4, 5, 7, **8**, 9, 38, 54, 55, 66, **68–97**, 105, 127, 128, 129, 131, **138–142**, 146, **152**
Royal Copley—see *Spaulding*
Royal Haeger—see *Haeger*
Rozane—see *Roseville*
R.R.P.Co.—see *Robinson Ransbottom*
RumRill, **97**
San Juan Pueblo—see *Native American*
Sandia Pueblo—see *Native American*
Santa Clara—see *Native American*
Saturday Evening Girls—see *S.E.G.*
Scio, 129
Sebring, **97–98**
S.E.G. (or Paul Revere), 8, **98**, **151**
Shawnee, **99**, 131
Shearwater, **99**
Silver Springs—see *H.A. Graack*
Spaulding (or Royal Copley), **99**
Stanford, **100**
Stangl, 30
Stonelain (or Associated American Artists), **100**
Strobl, 7, **100–101**, **153**
Sunrise, 8
Tamac, **101**
Tecate, 8
Teco (or Gates, or American Terra Cotta), 4, 30, **102**, **153**
Van Briggle, 4, 8, **103–104**, **142**, **153**
Wahpeton—see *Rosemeade*
Walley, J.W., 7, **104**
Weller, 4, 7, 8, 9, 15, 20, 38, 54, 66, **104–124**, 127, 128, 129–130, **143–145**, 146, **154–155**
Western Stoneware (or Monmouth), 8, **124–125**
Wheatley, 7, **125–126**, 127, **155**
White, 129
Wisecarver, Rick, **126**, **155**
Worthington, **126**, **144**
Zane—see *Peters and Reed*
Zanesville Stoneware, 128